THE INSIDE TRACK TO EXCELLING AS A BUSINESS ANALYST

SOFT SKILLS THAT CAN ACCELERATE YOUR CAREER

Roni Lubwama

Apress®

The Inside Track to Excelling As a Business Analyst: Soft Skills That Can Accelerate Your Career

Roni Lubwama
Spring, TX, USA

ISBN-13 (pbk): 978-1-4842-5542-1
https://doi.org/10.1007/978-1-4842-5543-8

ISBN-13 (electronic): 978-1-4842-5543-8

Managing Director, Apress Media LLC: Welmoed Spahr
Acquisitions Editor: Shiva Ramachandran
Development Editor: Rita Fernando
Coordinating Editor: Rita Fernando

Cover designed by eStudioCalamar

Distributed to the book trade worldwide by Springer Science+Business Media New York, 233 Spring Street, 6th Floor, New York, NY 10013. Phone 1-800-SPRINGER, fax (201) 348-4505, e-mail orders-ny@springer-sbm.com, or visit www.springeronline.com. Apress Media, LLC is a California LLC and the sole member (owner) is Springer Science + Business Media Finance Inc (SSBM Finance Inc). SSBM Finance Inc is a **Delaware** corporation.

For information on translations, please e-mail rights@apress.com, or visit http://www.apress.com/rights-permissions.

Apress titles may be purchased in bulk for academic, corporate, or promotional use. eBook versions and licenses are also available for most titles. For more information, reference our Print and eBook Bulk Sales web page at http://www.apress.com/bulk-sales.

Any source code or other supplementary material referenced by the author in this book is available to readers on GitHub via the book's product page, located at www.apress.com/9781484255421. For more detailed information, please visit http://www.apress.com/source-code.

Printed on acid-free paper

To GOD
For all the gifts He has given me.

To My Parents; George and Harriet Nsobya
For believing in me and instilling the "anything is possible" ethos that made this book possible.

To My Wife Sylvia and the Boys; Ethan, Rowan, Ryan and Shane
For the love, support and patience without which this book would not have succeeded.

To My Brothers and Sisters; Mirembe, Susan, Olivia, Philip and Mark
For believing in me, Stay Blessed!

To Ali Goljahmofrad
For opening my eyes to the world of writing and reviewing the book proposal.

To the Rockstars at Apress
Susan (for opening the door to Apress), Shiva and Rita; this work would not have seen the light of day without your professional and editorial oversight.

Contents

About the Author. vii

Introduction ix

Chapter 1: Business, Technology, and Change Management 1

Chapter 2: Business Analysts: What Do They Do?. 7

Chapter 3: Must-Have Technical Skills 27

Chapter 4: Optional Technical Skills 41

Chapter 5: Importance of Non-technical Skillsets 45

Chapter 6: Communication Skills 53

Chapter 7: Interpersonal Skills 79

Chapter 8: Creativity, Problem-Solving, and Strategic
Thinking Skills 111

Chapter 9: Business Analyst Practice Hacks 137

Chapter 10: When It's Time to Move On 145

Chapter 11: Afterword. 153

Appendix A: Bonus Skill: Managing Wafflers 155

Appendix B: Bonus Interpersonal Skill: Credibility and Reputation . . . 163

Appendix C: Further Reading 169

Index 175

About the Author

Roni Lubwama has more than 20 years of experience working in sales, marketing, logistics, and IT for major global organizations such as Shell Oil, Rackspace Inc., and Acumen Solutions. Over the past 6 years, he has worked as a Salesforce Business Systems Analyst and consultant on a number of Customer Relationship Management (CRM) digital transformation projects and initiatives. He is a University of Edinburgh MBA graduate who also holds Salesforce consultant certifications.

Roni lives in Houston, Texas with his wife Sylvia and their boys Ethan, Rowan, Ryan, and Shane. As an avid reader, he spends time reading about politics, history, culture, technology, economics, and sports, and he travels occasionally to Kampala, Uganda to connect with family and friends.

Introduction

"This job sucks!!"

If I earned a dollar each time I uttered this statement during my early Business Analyst days, I would be a millionaire. I found the job difficult, complex, and unrelentingly demanding. It seemed like every day presented a new fire I needed to put out. And fast.

To state that the learning curve was steep would be a gross understatement. However, this steep learning curve was flattened through a combination of self-study, mentoring, observation, and daily practice. These activities gave me the necessary business analyst skills I needed not only to survive but to thrive in complex and demanding project environments.

Once I was secure in the role, I observed how other newbies to the Business Analyst practice were experiencing the same pains I had gone through just a few months earlier.

This book is a modest exercise at "Paying it Forward" with the objective of sharing the knowledge I accumulated so that other Business Analysts can use it to excel at their careers. Think of the book as markers guiding you on a Business Analyst practice treasure hunt.

The techniques that I used to revive a promising but fledgling career will work for just about any profession and not just the Business Analyst practice. These techniques are detailed in later chapters, but for now, let's consider how you can make the most of this book.

Is This *the* Book for You?

How do I know if this is *the* Business Analyst book for you? I have no idea. That would be the realm of magic and I am no magician. But if any of the following questions have crossed your mind or have taken residence in your mind, then you're in the right place.

Fit is important in the things we commit to in life, and this book is no different. This chapter is compiled to enable you, the reader, gauge whether you and this book are a good fit. In no particular order, I review several scenarios that will establish whether you and this book are a great fit.

What Am I Going to Learn from This Book?

There are basic technical skills that a Business Analyst ought to have right out of the gate. We'll go over the details of what those technical skillsets are later in the book. Technical skills, however, are not the purpose of this book.

The theme of this book is to demonstrate the importance of non-technical skills and how Business Analysts (or other roles) can use them to achieve outstanding results on their assignments. This is not another self-help book repeatedly laced with hollow corporate buzzwords about leadership, blah blah, and the like. The concepts detailed here provide practical answers to the challenging daily realities Business Analysts (or other roles) regularly encounter in corporate and non-corporate settings.

Another Book About Business Analysts? Really?

What exactly is the point of writing another book about Business Analysts? After all, there are many books on this subject, and many more will be written. Where this little tome differs is that it gives the reader practical knowledge that can be applied to resolve real-life bottlenecks in corporate and non-corporate settings. It's not just another book; it's a handbook to get you through the hair-raising moments you are certain to encounter in the workplace.

What Do Business Analysts Do?

Ever wondered what Business Analysts do or how they do their jobs? Are you just curious or riled up by a Business Analyst on your team? This book will provide a structured explanation of the Business Analyst practice. That way you will have an explanation for why your Business Analyst is so annoying and what you *can* do about it.

I Would Like to Start a Business Analyst Career; Will This Book Help?

If yes, then the insights in this book will be useful. Note that I didn't mention a career in Business Analysis as many other roles do Business Analysis, yet they do not fall neatly into the Business Analyst role categorization. It's also worth noting that Business Analysts do a lot more than business analysis—which is the gist of this book. This book will not only help you understand what it takes to be a successful Business Analyst, it will also help you determine whether it's the role for you.

This book will also help you if you are changing careers or industries and moving to a Business Analyst role. For example, if you are a Food Scientist who would like to become a Business Analyst (happens more often than you think), this will make good reading for you.

That is the very purpose for which this book has been written. It gives ordinary Joes and Janes the tools they need to be successful Business Analysts when they are changing to a Business Analyst career.

Can This Book Help Me Get into the Tech Space?

Since Business Analysts are literally given the blueprints to any business process, they tend to have a bird's eye view of how businesses operate. They work closely with C-suite types (corporate speak for higher level executives), with run of the mill users who interface daily with technology products and with technical teams. This multifaceted exposure gives them an overview to myriad career paths and eventually allows many Business Analysts transition to senior roles on IT teams, Sales Operations, or even software product development teams. To my mind it's the best start one can get in tech given the exposure one gets to business operations and the many functional roles that make a business work. This book will show you what Business Analyst excellence looks like and with that a potentially good opening into the tech world.

I Am a New Business Analyst About to Be Exposed As an Impostor Will the Book Help Me?

Are you suffering from imposter syndrome?[1] Did you talk the Business Analyst talk during the interview, and its now time to walk the Business Analyst walk? You are in good hands. Just read the book. No questions asked; you will be grateful you did. This book is not a magic wand that will wipe away your lack of real-world experience. Nevertheless, if you hustle positively and apply these concepts, you will not only survive but you will also thrive in the competitive world that Business Analysts operate in.

---

[1] Imposter syndrome: When you have a deep-seated fear of being exposed as a fraud or know-nothing.

I Am Looking for a Resource That Will Improve My Business Analyst Craft

Take any role in the corporate workplace today and it is easy to feel challenged by the weight of responsibility that is placed on one's shoulders. If you feel like a Business Analyst role refresher could resolve the distress at hand, this book may be the refresher that you need. There is another reason to read this book: many of the concepts here are not taught (in this detail and context) in any Business Administration or Computer Science course. This book will detail a coherent and structured pathway that can enable one to succeed as a Business Analyst in any corporate setting.

As a Business Analyst There Are Too Many Fires to Put Out; I Need Practical Answers

This is for the Business Analyst wondering whether these concepts are indeed magic bullets to some of the issues vexing them in their Business Analyst role. These concepts *will* help you slay those dragons if applied suitably and consistently. I didn't slap these concepts together on a languid Texas summer afternoon; rather I meticulously put them together after working with some of the best Business Analysts in the business. Stop the doubting and start the reading; you will thank me for it.

I Am Not a Techie, I Just Need a Resource to Help Navigate Workplace Issues

While the book references the tech world and specifically the software product development process, these concepts are universal and can be applied to many roles in both corporate and noncorporate settings. If things in your current role are going sideways, then this book will be a good start with helping you dig yourself out of the hole you are in.

I Am an Experienced Business Analyst; Why Do I Need This Book?

For the Business Analyst maestros out there, reading this book will provide you with new insights and approaches to sticky issues native to the Business Analyst practice. More importantly you can "pay it forward" by recommending this book to other pratitioners of the Business Anayst trade. Any ideas to improve the book are also more than welcome.

How to Get the Most from This Book

Business Analysts operate in a vast change management ecosystem that continues to evolve with the constantly shifting business and information technology landscapes. Thriving professionally in these environments requires a finely tuned set of skills that can be precisely deployed to match these fluid environments.

This book illustrates what those skillsets are and how they can be applied by Business Analysts to achieve change management objectives. More specifically this book will highlight how Business Analysts use non-technical skillsets to successfully manage their assignments. To achieve that objective, this is how the book is structured:

Chapter 1: Business, Technology, and Change Management

The main purpose of this chapter is to introduce the world of the Business Analyst to the reader by detailing the how and what of the Business Analyst role. You can think of this section as an introduction to Business Analyst foundational principles.

The chapter also reviews the intersection of business, technology, change management, and the Business Analyst connection.

Chapter 2: Business Analysts: What Do They Do?

This chapter reviews the definition of the Business Analyst practice as well as what Business Analysts do. Understanding what Business Analysts do sets the foundation that equips one to understand what excellence in this business looks like.

It also considers at a macro-level software product development methodologies and processes. These principles are important as they set the stage for determining which skillsets a Business Analyst requires for a software product development phase and why. While it is not essential to go into the weeds where these processes are concerned, it is important to to understand what they are as that provides insights into how they impact the Business Analyst practice.

Chapters 3–11: Technical and Non-Technical Skillsets for Business Analysts

The remaining chapters of this book provide a high level rundown of required technical skills for Business Analysts. These are the types of skills any Business Analyst would be expected to have at the commencement of any assignment. They are the basics for the Business Analyst role.

More importantly, these chapters lay out the importance of non-technical skills and how Business Analysts can use them to elevate their performance levels. It is non-technical skills that enable a Business Analyst to stand out by consistently delivering exceptional results. This is where it all comes together for it reviews how Business Analysts use multifaceted non-technical skills to deliver complex change management demands.

Lastly, this section details some "hacks" that are used by Business Analyst practitioners to deliver their assignments and it ends by reviewing assignments that cannot be salvaged as well as when it is time to move on.

Appendices A and B: Bonus Skills

At the end of this book, I provide coverage of additional non-technical bonus skills.

Whatever Floats Your Boat

There are no hard and fast rules to getting the most from this book. Gauge your interest, assess your goals and objectives for getting this book, and get on the train at any stop that suits you. If you can do it chronologically from start to finish, that's great for you. If you consider the references to be what will cut it for you, then by all means be my guest.

Happy reading!

Business, Technology, and Change Management

The Business Analyst Connection

To fully understand the world of the Business Analyst, we need to first comprehend the forces and environments that drive the world Business Analysts operate in. With this high-level foundation, we are in a position to understand where, how, and why the Business Analyst fits into this landscape.

The Need for Change

Business organizations operate in competitive environments, and they realize that adopting novel technologies can and does impart competitive advantages to first movers.

© Roni Lubwama 2020
R. Lubwama, *The Inside Track to Excelling As a Business Analyst*,
https://doi.org/10.1007/978-1-4842-5543-8_1

In a roundabout way, there is very little upside to staying analogue. Consider the fact that the combination of connectivity and mobility technologies means that very few of us need to actually go to a physical bank to conduct bank-related transactions. Those tasks are seamlessly done by our mobile devices.

The drive—generated by market forces—to transition from manual processes to analogue to digital is the transformation that many business organizations seek when they undertake technological changes to the way they operate. These technological changes in organizations are commonly referred to as digital transformation initiatives, and they are usually rolled out via the change management discipline.

Change Management

Change management is a structured approach to managing the transformation of an organization's operations, processes, or technologies. Change management is not a mindless management exercise (though sometimes it appears to be); it is directly related to the achievement and fulfillment of organizational goals. Changing business processes, changing process architecture, optimizing redundant assets, or the introduction of new software products are examples of organizational transformation goals that can be achieved by the overarching umbrella that is change management.

Change Management and Technology Products

In today's technological landscape, the most sought-after technologies have not only changed the way organizations work but also how customers interact with those organizations. These technological platforms and products are in demand clearly because they confer competitive advantages and efficiency gains to the organizations that have integrated them into their operations.

Let's consider some in-demand technologies that have caused tectonic shifts in the way business organizations operate today.

- **Mobility**

  As mobile devices have become ubiquitous, so have the business transactions conducted on those devices. This has led to the growth of mobile apps and associated technologies to support this ecosystem. It has become a *must-have* platform for most organizations.

- ## Digital Marketplaces

  Business transactions are no longer the domain of brick-and-mortar shops. Meaning, a significant portion of what usually needed to be done in physical stores can now be done online in an instant. Web technologies have grown in response to this need, and they not only support transactions but they also provide technologies that determine how products are sold and marketed online.

- ## Analytics and Business Intelligence

  Data collection and storage do not confer competitive advantage by themselves, but it is the interpretation of that data that businesses organizations are most interested in.

- ## Cloud Computing

  It used to be that starting a business or building a web application required an upfront investment in IT infrastructure like servers. The transition to cloud computing and the rapid growth of cloud data storage largely eliminated that need. Businesses and applications can be built in the cloud in a matter of hours with next-to-zero investment in hardware.

- ## Business Process Reengineering

  Remember the days when business processes meant actual paper pushing? Not anymore. Changing how processes work or how they are architected is a key objective of any digital transformation initiative with the intent of unlocking efficiencies, cost reduction, and waste elimination among other related process improvement benefits.

- ## 24/7 Connectivity

  Why should a business go to sleep in one part of the world when in another part of the world, customers are lining up to buy its products? Telecommunications technologies have unleashed novel ways in which we communicate and connect with each other. Today, there are many global businesses where physical borders are things of the past given that communications are now almost seamless round the clock.

- **Artificial Intelligence and Machine Learning**

    Unbelievable as it sounds, the term artificial intelligence was coined in the 1950s, and at the time of this publication, it has gained maturity to the point where we use it daily. Aside from the mundane, like verbal commands to your thermostat, it has powerful applications in businesses where it can be used to make accurate insights and predictions pertaining to real-time business operations

It is these and many more technological innovations that form the backbone of many organizational digital transformation initiatives.

Another thing about these technologies is that they are in demand by non-profit organizations as well; it's not just profit-oriented organizations that utilize these technologies. It is not unheard of for nonprofit organizations to undergo the same digital transformation initiatives that for-profit organizations are zealously seeking to undertake. After all, if the customers of non-profits have made the digital transition, why would they respond to organizations using analogue means to engage them?

For many of these technological products, you can flip a couple of switches to fire them up after acquisition. However, if these products are required to work with other software products as well as have a footprint in disparate parts of a business organization, then merely flipping switches may not be very productive.

This juncture is where we need to work with the change management discipline and its cousin project management. What these disciplines do is enable organizations to work with structured road maps that guide the implementation of technology products while ensuring that the targeted benefits are realized.

So, what do Business Analysts have to do with this primer about business and technology?

The Business Analyst Connection

Where exactly does a Business Analyst fit into the business, technology, and change management discussions?

It may sound clichéd to state that Business Analysts sit at the intersection of business operations, technology, and change management, but it is a clichéd truth. Business organizations need technology products, and change management is the vehicle by which technology products are rolled out in organizations. As you might have guessed, Business Analysts working in concert with other stakeholders are driving that vehicle to deliver the objectives of digital transformation initiatives.

Change management by itself cannot deliver a digital transformation initiative; it usually works in tandem with the project management discipline to deliver those objectives.

Consider project management the sidekick of change management; the former is concerned with the tasks, process, and tools that deliver digital transformation, while the latter is more concerned with who and what gets impacted by digital transformation initiatives. In a few words where you have change management, you will likely *have* project management. See Figure 1-1.

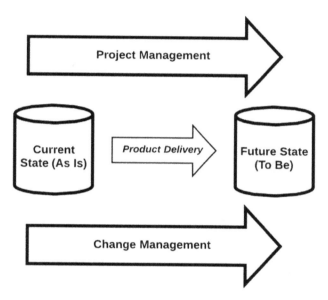

Figure 1-1. Change Management and Project Management

To that end, in order to deliver a digital transformation initiative, you need to apply change management and project management principles. In furtherance of this objective, most project setups require an embedded Business Analyst so that they can be the frontline resource for assessing business needs and facilitating the eventual success of a digital transformation initiative.

How Business Analysts execute on these seemingly blurry deliverables is the subject of the next chapters.

Business Analysts: What Do They Do?

Business Analysts in corporate settings come in many flavors, and they work in a wide variety of industries, verticals, and domains. Given that goals, objectives, and structures differ from organization to organization, the designation and actual work content of a Business Analyst will accordingly differ as well.

The naming conventions of the Business Analyst role can be mind-boggling for it is not uncommon for Business Analysts to be referred to as Change Managers, Business Process Analysts, Business System Analysts, Consultants, and Business Process Managers.

If the naming conventions for mere designations appear designed to confuse, then consider how even more confusing the job description of a Business Analyst can be from one organization to the next. The reality is that even though Business Analysts may be called many colorful names or execute a variety of tasks, the essence of the role remains the same which is to facilitate change management in the technology space. More specifically, Business Analysts are in the business of delivering business processes and technology products that bring value to end users.

© Roni Lubwama 2020
R. Lubwama, *The Inside Track to Excelling As a Business Analyst*,
https://doi.org/10.1007/978-1-4842-5543-8_2

Business Analyst Definition

A Business Analyst in the tech world is essentially a go-between or intermediary between two parties in an organization. For instance, if you the reader need to acquire and roll out a new software product or if you need to change a troublesome business process, these requests are channeled to a Business Analyst for analytical review.

After this review is complete, the Business Analyst works with another part of your organization to deliver what you requested. That other part of your organization can be your IT, Business Intelligence, Analytics, or Procurement departments.

This simplified description is at the heart of what Business Analysts do in any organizational transformation initiative.

Why Do You Need to Work with a Business Analyst?

Do you have to work with a Business Analyst during a digital transformation initiative? That would depend on your organizational structure, goals, and objectives, but it is best practice to embed a resource who will undertake the role of a Business Analyst. Whatever designation you give this person, they will be a critical cog in your change processes.

If you are changing the way you work, the way you access your customers, or the way data is managed in your organization, you are going to need a Business Analyst of some sort. This resource is there to evaluate the needs inherent in the digital transformation initiative as well facilitate the delivery of those changes. There are many cogs and contributors that deliver successful digital transformation initiatives, and a Business Analyst is just one of those cogs albeit a very important one.

The Future of the Business Analyst Role

Make no mistake, Business Analysts are a critical anchor in any digital transformation initiatives and change management processes.

For as long as digital transformation initiatives and change management are required by organizations, a Business Analyst—or a similar resource—will be a part of that discussion.

Does the Business Analyst practice have a place in the technologies of the future? I don't know if there are many crystal balls that would give us a precise answer, but it's clear human beings will be needed to build and architect those new technologies.

New technologies?

That looks and sounds a lot like change management, and as you might have already guessed, this means the presence of Business Analysts of some sort or flavor. Besides, the last time I checked, soft skills like communication and emotional intelligence are not robots and algorithms strong points. This role will not be going the way of the dodo anytime soon.

We now know who a Business Analyst is but what do they do?

What Do Business Analysts Do?

What constitutes the work content for a Business Analyst, and what are the deliverables expected of them? In this business understanding, the end destination of the journey is a crucial input for any initiative undertaken by a Business Analyst. The question "What does success look like?" is heard frequently for the simple reason it assesses at any point in time what the destination looks like when viewed from where you stand.

The work of Business Analysts generally falls into these categories, and while the categorizations differ from one organization or project to another, the general outline here remains the same.

Problem or Pain Point Identification

It may sound odd, but one of the key roles of a Business Analyst is to basically "finger" a problem with certainty. Through what are called discovery sessions, they must be confident in stating that A, B, and C are the problems and not X, Y, and Z as may be assumed. To this end Business Analysts must master the art of asking questions for this is how they get answers to both known and unknown questions. It is also how they validate prevailing assumptions in organizations.

Think of the last time your organization made major changes to the way you worked. There was an irritating person who asked questions about *anything and everything*. As examples, he/she was interested in knowing what you do, how you did it, and if you had any improvements to suggest. They may have been irritating, but there was a method and purpose to the irritation as will be detailed later.

Requirements—An Introduction

Once the Business Analyst has identified the issues, they need to put the issue before the technical resources who will devise solutions to eradicate the end user pain points.

How is this done?

A Business Analyst accomplishes this by using requirements. At a high level, a requirement is a description of end user needs or expectations from a software product or component.

Requirements like Business Analysts go by many names, and a few like requirements specifications, software requirements specifications, functional specifications, business requirements, and many others come to mind.

A requirement is merely the vehicle through which the identified issue will be resolved, and all it does is specify details of the issue that need to be remedied.

Some organizations and project setups require that a requirement be heavily detailed, while others request that the requirement be minimally detailed. On the other end of the spectrum are organizations and project setups that require their requirements to have the *barest* of details. All the requirement has to state is the need and the purpose of that need.[1]

How detailed a requirement will be is also a function of the methodology[2] in use on a product development project.

Requirements Elicitation

It is the process of seeking to understand at a deeper level the issues impacting end users who have flagged those issues as problems requiring urgent resolution. Requirements elicitation—which is used interchangeably with requirements gathering—at its most basic level seeks to understand as much context and background about the problem as possible. From the elicitation process, a Business Analyst will proceed to develop or draft requirements.

During the elicitation process, a Business Analyst will spend time with end users seeking to understand concepts like

- *How* many users are encountering this problem? How *often* and *when?*

- Where is the *data* that speaks to these assertions? Is it *verifiable?*

---

[1] This is usually the case with Agile requirements or user stories.
[2] Software Development Methodologies are covered later in this chapter

As you may have noticed by the highlighted words, the Business Analyst is building a watertight case out of the interactions with the end users who flagged the issue. The intent is to build requirements that can withstand the rigors of technical reviews by project team members, and it is generally good practice to write requirements that are based on verifiable data and assumptions.

As a Business Analyst, if your requirements cannot pass muster during technical reviews, then you probably need to better validate the assumptions and data underlying the requirements.

Drafting valid and verifiable requirements from end users is a key part of Business Analyst deliverables, and it forms a significant portion of their work content as well as deliverables.

Requirements Documentation

Depending on the project or organizational setup, requirements are firmed up in a Business Requirement Document (BRD) or a Requirements Specification Document (RSD) or whatever it is called.

The BRD is essentially documentation that states the problem (as is) and what the future state (to be) will look like when the requirements are implemented.

Usually it lists the requirements in a structured format that includes the problem, the context or background, the assumptions, the requirements, and in some cases the technical solutions to the identified problems.

The BRD by its very nature is a one-trick pony, and it focuses on specific problems and the need for resolutions for *those problems*. It's just another name for the scope of the requirements, and it references what those requirements will resolve and by implication what those requirements will not resolve (or even think about resolving).

Some organizations and project setups require an approved BRD or merely signed-off requirements before proceeding to devise a technical solution to the problem. In these instances, the approvals are granted by end users or project leadership with the approval basically confirming that the issue has been identified and that these requirements will enable correction of the issue.

Requirements Sign-Offs

Securing signed-off requirements may sound like a run-of-the-mill task in the requirement management process, but it is a major milestone fraught with myriad implications.

It is the role of Business Analysts to secure requirements sign-offs, and the reason why it is a delicate milestone comes down to ownership and account-ability. By agreeing to requirements, end users are putting reputations on the line by endorsing changes that may or may not be successful when considered as part of a larger transformation initiative.

Likewise, it's also an endorsement by Business Analysts that they approve the changes requested by end users. If the changes in the BRD do not produce the intended results, any root cause analysis (RCA)[3] is certain to come back to this point in time to ascertain causes of failure.

For purposes of retrospective accountability, Business Analysts must consider a requirements' sign-off with clear-eyed professionalism.

Support to Solution Providers and End Users

You are now done with the requirements so what comes next? Those require-ments are semi-specifications used to develop or acquire a technology prod-uct that provides a solution to end users who raised the requirement with a Business Analyst.

While the technical teams design and develop the product requested by the requirements, Business Analysts are the go-to people for any information gaps that are uncovered by these processes. The technical team may want to know for instance whether a requirement is referring to X or Y, which is where the Business Analyst steps in with clarifications.

Remember the part about the Business Analyst being an intermediary? This is one of the points when they get to play that role.

At other times end users need to understand how a solution they requested works which is the responsibility of the Business Analyst to provide training and guidance.

The work of a Business Analyst does not stop at identifying the problem and drafting requirements: their input is required for as long as the process of crafting and delivering a functional solution is still ongoing.

Definition of Success for Business Analysts

How is the success of a Business Analyst measured? How is this success quan-tified? The inputs of a Business Analyst and subsequent deliverables at a very basic level come down to whether they delivered what end users asked for. Two examples come to mind.

---

[3] Root cause analysis: A discipline that analyzes causes of failure and mitigation measures to prevent repeat failure events.

Business Process Improvement

All organizations have business processes with redundant and unreasonable kinks. Sometimes a project seeks to straighten out these imperfections, and it should be visible to end users that they have fewer steps (or none) to perform previously tedious tasks. A project that creates more steps or marginally improves the previous business process does not count as a successful deliverable.

Productivity and Efficiency Improvements

Successfully automating mundane clerical tasks provides productivity and efficiency gains to end users. An initiative that seeks to create efficiencies but leaves end users with merely incremental changes to the previous workflows does not count as a wildly successful change either.

Obviously, the Business Analyst does not build, design, and test the product by themselves; but their input by way of precise requirements and project support is critical to delivering a functional product for end users.

Despite a project being staffed by many other roles, it is important to note that all these roles largely work on and deliver inputs provided by Business Analysts or a resource who performs this role.

There are many other factors—internal or external—like resource deficits or corporate politics that derail projects, but it is always clear as day when a project is derailed due to inadequate requirements management.

The definition of Business Analyst success varies from organization to organization, but ultimately most organizations and project setups assess whether requirements delivered what end users asked for. This is a good place to start when seeking to define what success looks like for Business Analysts.

Tools and Methodologies Business Analysts Work With

The delivery of software projects is governed by structured methodologies. These methodologies play a significant role in how Business Analysts meet their deliverables. A brief primer on how these methodologies work sets the foundation for understanding how these factors influence the success of a Business Analyst.

Project Management Structures

Project management structures of some sort or variation are the vehicles of choice for most organizations as they seek to deliver software products to end users. These projects operate with defined and approved scopes, timelines, and budgets.

A project could run anywhere from 1 to 36 months with many more subprojects with differing timelines nested inside the major project. As an example, an organization that is rolling out new staffing and human resources applications would plan to deliver this project in approximately 12 months with the possibility of extensions if roadblocks that lead to delays are encountered.

An initiative of this reach and impact would call for setting up a Project Management Office (PMO) to deliver it per approved scope, timeline, and budget. Project work is broken down into assignments, tasks, and sub-tasks that are split into Sprints[4] (if using Agile) or phases/sub-phases (if using Waterfall).[5]

PMOs can be set up as a one-person show (only a Project Manager) or a fully-fledged autonomous sub-department that staffs projects, monitors project implementation, and provides project-related reporting.

For Business Analysts the PMO is just another beast that they need to manage during project execution. A surefire way for a Business Analyst to get a project into trouble is to underestimate the role they need to play in project management.

Unlike project budgets, Business Analysts have direct influence over the scope and timelines of a project. More specifically, requirements delivered by Business Analysts determine the scope of the solution and by ensuring that those requirements are developed within set timelines they exert control over project timeframes as well.

It is for this reason that many organizations require Business Analysts who are conversant with or have prior experience with project management.

The Software Development Life Cycle (SDLC)

Software development is a delicate process which requires sound software development practices and rigorous testing before it is released to end users or the general public (if it is customer-facing).

Wonder why when you click some web pages, they open blank pages or sometimes you get a 404-error message when the same page was working just seconds ago? Chances are that is the result of poor software development work or insufficient testing that did not expose the glitch. It is for this reason that the development and release of software use a methodology known as the SDLC to govern this process.

---

[4] Incremental and iterative time-boxed periods used to plan, design, and develop software products using the Agile Software Development Methodology.
[5] Waterfall: a linear sequential-based methodology for Software Development.

The SDLC or Software Development Life Cycle has four key milestones: Plan, Design, Development, and Test (and Deploy). Organizations and projects use the SDLC as it suits them, but generally they work around delivering software that has gone through the plan, design, build, and test phases.

No prizes for guessing, but Business Analysts are going to be involved in each of these phases. They may be heavily involved, for example, in the planning phase and have light involvement in the development phase. The level of effort that a Business Analyst puts into a phase will be determined by the project setup or organizational expectations.

For clarity, Business Analysts will plan/scope the needs of the project, assist with input for the design/development phases, and support the testing/rollout phases. Each of these phases has its own unique demands, and Business Analysts need to be cognizant of which skillsets to deploy in order to support a phase of this cycle. Those skillsets are what the proceeding chapters will detail.

Software Development Methodology

The Software Development Life Cycle is also governed by the mode of execution during the delivery of software products. Think of this as the route by which the product is delivered.

The Waterfall Approach

One approach, the Waterfall approach—and the original one—is to collect all the requirements up front, develop the product, test it, and release it all in *one* effort. It is a sequential approach that moves from one phase to another, and a new phase cannot be started unless the previous one has been signed off as successfully completed (Figure 2-1). For example, requirements need to be fully compiled, signed off, and approved at the end of the planning phase before the design phase can start.

It is not unusual for this approach to take 6 or 24 months.

Remember the route analogy previously described? Waterfall is about setting of from point A to point C by moving straight through points A, B, and C step by step—in linear fashion.

The Waterfall approach works best when all the requirements are known, and once a project is flagged off, new requirements cannot be incorporated in the project.

In a nutshell, it is a very inflexible approach to work with. But what happens if end users want to change requirements or customers request more changes to the software product as the project is in motion? These questions and inflexibilities set the stage for the development of another approach.

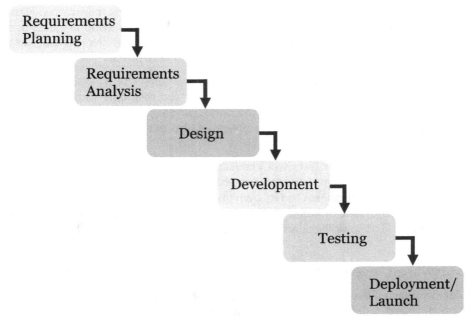

Figure 2-1. The Waterfall Methodology

The Agile/Scrum Approach

The second and recently more popular approach is the Agile/Scrum approach. It essentially realizes that end user and customer needs can change and a software product that was required last year may not be needed in the same format, type, or functionality this year.

Agile is cognizant of these changes and the need for flexibility in the software development process. Agile also acknowledges the ambiguity that comes with end user requirements by recognizing the fact that some projects will not know *all* the product requirements at the start of a new project. This acknowledgment essentially accepts continuous requirements evolution, uncovering of new requirements, and the inclusion of those new requirements in the scope as the project continues to move forward.

The point of Agile is to enable a project to evolve its requirements as it proceeds which provides requirements flexibility during the life cycle of the project.

It is a very flexible mode of software development with an increasing number of project setups and organizations now using Agile or a Hybrid Agile methodology. In a recent survey of 1,300 organizations conducted by CollabNet VersionOne, 97% of the respondents reported that their organizations practiced Agile development methods.[6]

---

[6]www.stateofagile.com/#ufh-i-423641583-12th-annual-state-of-agile-report/473508

The Agile way uses short development cycles or iterations to deliver software products (for our purposes we will refer to them as iterations or sprints). These iterations each have a plan, design, build, test, and deploy cycle with a duration of 2, 4, and 6 weeks. Think of Agile with iterations as the mini Waterfalls. See Figure 2-2.

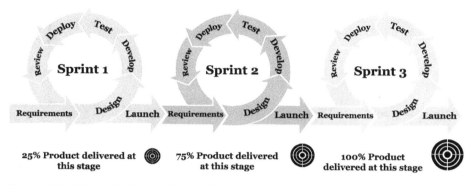

Figure 2-2. The Agile Methodology and Sprint Iterations

There are other software development methodologies that are spin-offs from Agile or are hybrids of both Agile and Waterfall, but these two are the prominent methodologies in use.

Organizational needs, experiences, and skillsets ultimately determine which direction an organization takes when it comes to methodologies to use during the product development process.

But how is a Business Analyst involved with all this techy-sounding stuff?

If Business Analysts are going to manage requirements and support the product development cycle effectively, then they need to understand how software development methodologies work.

Given that software development methodologies work differently, it is important to understand how these differences impact the outputs of a Business Analyst. For instance, Agile emphasizes "working software over comprehensive documentation"[7] which means less requirements documentation that also delivers functional software products. See Figure 2-3.

These are subtle distinctions, but they impact Business Analyst deliverables as detailed in the coming chapters.

---

[7] Agile manifesto: https://agilemanifesto.org/

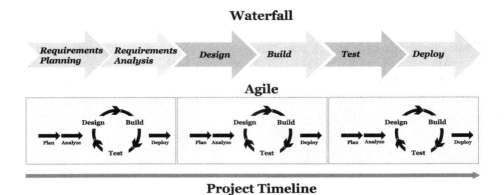

Figure 2-3. Comparison Between Waterfall and Agile Methodologies

Case Study: ABC Corp

How about laying out a real-life case study that illustrates how these concepts come together? More importantly, how about an illustration that shows the Business Analyst's place in this universe?

Consider a company I am familiar with from another life: ABC Corp, a multinational corporation lacking a sales and customer service management system. A situation that has given rise to these dysfunctional business processes:

1. Sales representatives routinely chase the same customer and in a few embarrassing situations encounter each other at customer's premises trying to sell the same product to the same customer.

2. Customers requesting support often never hear back from the company. Their customer support departments are walled off from sales and manufacturing.

3. Sales figures reported to executives are either underestimated or are wildly exaggerated.

4. Sales projections are not backed by verifiable data as a unified platform for forecasting and reporting does not exist.

5. A major issue they are facing is that customer data belongs to employees and not the company. When an employee leaves the company, that data walks out the door with that employee. There is no central platform that tracks which activities an employee is engaged in with a specific customer.

ABC Corp is aware of these teething problems and realizes that they are only going to get worse as the company scales. To eliminate these process nightmares, ABC Corp undertakes the implementation and rollout of a software application that supports sales enablement, manages customer data, and provides customer service support.

There are many applications and software products that cater to these needs ranging from enterprise-grade applications to simple software products that cater to pop and mom outfits. For our purposes we will assume that ABC Corp is purchasing an enterprise software product that it will use to improve its business processes and operations.

Which begs the question, what's the point of using project management to turn on a ready-to-go software product? We might as well just flip a switch, and the application is ready for use by end users.

The simple reason is that an "out of the box"[8] software product will not meet all the needs of users and functions in an organization. Lest we forget, different end users require different functionality from the software product. While it is the same software product, it can be configured to enable different users perform different tasks in different parts of an organization.

It is these changes, configurations, and customizations that are managed through the Software Development Life Cycle using either Waterfall or Agile methodology.

Among other project-related needs, ABC Corp needs a Project Charter or Project Plan. They also need the project set up focused on delivering an Agile project. The specifics of these two items are as follows:

- **Project Charter (or a Project Plan)**

    This document provides overall project governance. It provides justification for the rollout, project milestones, technical milestones (like integrations), deliverables, and definition of success.

- **Software Development Methodology**

    Given that the scope of deliverables is not fully known and that needs of the end users are likely to keep evolving, this initiative will use Agile as a software development methodology.

---

[8] Out of the box (OOTB) software products: prepackaged software that comes with standard functionality that will meet general end user needs. Specific end user needs require the opposite of OOTB products which is customized or bespoke products.

The SDLC is going to be meshed with the Agile Software Development Methodology in order to create a lean and nimble project framework.

This project will use a two-week sprint cadence as part of Agile project management. This two-week sprint encompasses requirements planning, product design, product development, and testing. Requirements that are undeveloped[9] after the two-week sprint are carried over to the next sprint. The finished product is released or deployed as specified in the project plan, and that is either at the end of a given number of sprints or at regular weekly or monthly intervals.

This is a highly simplified walk-through of how Agile project management works, but for our purposes, it clarifies Agile project management vis à vis the Business Analysts role in that process.

Requirements Planning and Analysis

Business Analysts farm out to the different users and departments and compile requirements preferably weeks before the first sprint starts.

ABC Corp will benefit from an Agile approach for they do not have the time to compile all the requirements up front nor do they know what the bulk of those requirements are going to be.

When those initial requirements are complete, the first sprint cycles commence, and as those sprints are in motion, the Business Analysts continue the requirements elicitation process.

Business Analysts also use the sprints to filter out more end user needs that will be plugged into future sprints as new requirements.

This is usually done when end users are shown the product during the design, development, and testing phases. At each of these touchpoints, end users can point out new requests which are logged in a requirements backlog. These new requests eventually become new requirements for upcoming sprints.

If end users are satisfied with the requirements, then they are signed off as complete and ready for review by the technical team.

What to Watch For

- Requirements elicitation is an ongoing process even when sprints are in motion.

---

[9] Undeveloped: not all requirements planned for development in a sprint will be developed. Some requirements will need to be carried over to the next sprint if they require a larger development effort.

- Business Analysts need to become Subject Matter Experts (SMEs) for the processes they seek to change. You cannot champion change if you do not understand why the change is required in the first place.

- Deep understanding of the business processes involved in order to sequence what requirements get worked on first and why.

Design Phase

Requirements review sessions are complete, and the technical team takes a stab at designing a product based on the requirements.

The nerds on the team develop a prototype of the component or product requested by the requirement. They can either demonstrate[10] the prototype to stakeholders or proceed with actual product development.

What to Watch For

- Business Analysts mainly play a supporting role during product design.

- The design team may require clarification on requirements. The Business Analyst will play the role of Subject Matter Expert and provide clarity as may be requested. Mostly, Business Analysts plug any information gaps that are exposed by the design process.

- Expect a bit of back and forth in terms of clarifications as the design process goes full throttle.

- Expect to enter negotiations with end users if the design team develops a design that has technical limitations (the finished product does not always deliver *all* the requested bells and whistles). The negotiations are intended to check end user acceptance of a "limited" product or whether there is an acceptable workaround[11] for the limitation.

---

[10] Product Demonstration, also known as a Demo, is when technical teams demonstrate a prototype to project stakeholders.

[11] Workaround: a temporary (though sometimes longer term) fix that works as a solution to a software and hardware limitation or shortcoming.

Product Development

The product takes shape in this phase.

Technical teams (more specifically software developers) configure or use code to develop the software product and its component functionality as specified in the requirements. The technical team will conduct tests on the developed product to check that the software product works as specified in the requirements. After testing they can either demo the product or move it to quality assurance engineers for different types of specialized testing.

What to Watch For

- Just like in the design phase, Business Analysts mainly play a supporting role during product development.

- The development team may require clarification on requirements that are unclear. As a Subject Matter Expert, the Business Analyst's role is to provide feedback or source the feedback requested by the technical team.

- Expect some back and forth as the software development team builds the product.

- If the development process turns up a technical hurdle that prevents the development of a component that was requested by a requirement, expect to negotiate this hurdle with end users. The objective of the negotiations is to secure their buy-in to use a product that does not deliver 100% of the requested requirement. Either seek that buy-in or sell end users a workaround option.

Test Phase

Quality assurance engineers run different tests for the developed product components. Those tests among others check product performance, functionality, and integrations with other applications. Once these tests are signed off as successful, then end user testing or User Acceptance Testing (UAT) can commence.

It is best practice for Business Analysts to conduct testing before User Acceptance Testing starts.

To that end Business Analysts test the developed product to validate that what has been developed matches what was requested by end users in the requirements.

Business Analysts also conduct testing before end user testing in order to catch any glitches or defects. Any defects uncovered by Business Analysts are brought to the attention of the technical team for correction.

When testing is cleared as successful by Business Analysts, then User Acceptance Testing commences.

End users get to test the software product derived from the requirements that were submitted to the Business Analyst. In effect they run the same tests as Business Analysts, and among other things, they will test for functionality, performance, look and feel, and data flows (integrations) with other applications.

When end users are satisfied that the product works as intended, then UAT is considered successful and the product is ready to be released or deployed.

If they encounter defects, the defective components are recycled into the development process, corrected, UATd again, and signed off as successful.

But what happens if the product is not just glitchy but is different from what was requested in the requirements? This is not an ideal situation and not one you want to deal with, but it happens from time to time.

It is resolved by drafting new requirements and pressing them into the design, development, and test cycle. This is an oversimplification of what happens, but this scenario covers many messy moving parts like justifications for the changes, requests for extra budget, and requests to extend timelines, to name a few. I would avoid these scenarios like the plague.

What to Watch For

- Expect more involvement in testing as a Business Analyst especially before end user testing (UAT).

- If you delivered technically concise requirements, then testing will be a breeze and the product will work as expected.

- Conversely if the requirements were unclear and the development teams didn't seek clarity, don't be surprised if the product does not match the requirements you drafted.

Deployment

Also known as Go Live or Product Launch, the product is made available to end users for use in their daily work activities. Business Analysts still have some heavy lifting to do during product launch.

Deployment takes many forms, and there are many back-end technical activities that take place during this phase.

What to Watch For

- Expect to provide support for launch activities like end user training either in person or by working with a training vendor.

- Provide documentation and user guides for the released products.

- Document technical activities undertaken by the development teams for instance data mappings.

Post-deployment Activities

It is tempting to consider the work of a Business Analyst complete once a software product is deployed and end users are working with it daily.

It doesn't work this way.

There are activities that still require the involvement of a Business Analyst long after the product is deployed to end users.

What to Watch For

- Expect to monitor product usage, adoption, and usage metrics.

- The need to devise strategies that improve end user usage of the application. These strategies may be based on triaging issues that are preventing end users from adopting the product.

- Legacy applications in IT parlance are applications that are being replaced or no longer in use. Business Analysts provide documentation pertaining to the decommissioning of legacy applications. Expect to support technical teams as they archive data and migrate data from legacy applications prior to decommissioning.

- Provide end user training as may be required.

- Managing defects and glitches that arise from daily use of the product. Usually they are placed on a fast track for correction and deployed to users as soon as they are corrected.

- Take on end user ideas and recommendations for improvements. These ideas are recycled as requirements for future sprints.

This is a typical Agile software development implementation that illustrates the responsibilities of Business Analysts during the different phases of the Software Development Life Cycle (SDLC).

Organizations are different, and each will execute software product development in a way that best suits its objectives, resources, and skillsets. Nevertheless, this case study is a broad outline of how a software product is developed and deployed as well as the Business Analysts' place in that process.

Business Analysts undertake many overt as well as behind the scenes activities in order to bring digital transformation initiatives across the finishing line. The tools and skillsets Business Analysts use to get across that finishing line are the subject of the next chapters.

Must-Have Technical Skills

Business Analysts need technical skills so that they can scope requirements and support the Software Development Life Cycle. Some technical skills or knowledge like how databases function is obviously more important than whether as a Business Analyst you can write code.

Do your competencies need to be above average for all the skills detailed here? The answer would be yes for some technical skills like technical writing and no for others like programming or coding skills. Keep in mind that the distinction as to whether a given set of skills is more critical than another set on a software development project is largely governed by project and organizational management. This setup determines what technical skills a Business Analyst should have, a case in point being projects that require Six Sigma certifications for their Business Analysts.

Like most roles in the information technology universe, the technical skills required to accomplish Business Analyst assignments will always be subject to the vagaries of change.

It is not a given that many of these technical skills and the way we use them will still be needed years from now; that's not how the information technology ecosystem functions. What we can be certain of, however, is that they will still be in use albeit in different formats and how they will be applied.

© Roni Lubwama 2020
R. Lubwama, *The Inside Track to Excelling As a Business Analyst*,
https://doi.org/10.1007/978-1-4842-5543-8_3

An example that illustrates this concept is the requirement for Business Analysts to be adept at using data querying tools like Scripted Query Language (SQL) when I was first hired as a Business Analyst many eons ago. In the intervening period, I have observed many Business Analysts accomplish deeply impactful software development projects without ever writing one SQL query. This can partly be explained by the fact that technological innovations keep churning out new data management tools that can accomplish data analysis without using SQL.

Another caveat to point out is that a Business Analyst is not going to use all these technical skills at the same time on the same project. Different projects have different requirements that call for the deployment of some technical skills, while others may be considered irrelevant for that project. Nevertheless, there are must-have skills like technical writing, use cases application, and analytical skills among others that are required by a Business Analyst for any software development project.

In this chapter, we focus on the technical skills Business Analysts must have.

General Document Skills

What do you use to compile requirements documentation? Microsoft Word. How about requirements sessions and presentations? Microsoft PowerPoint. Number crunching and data analysis? Microsoft Excel. Flowcharting and diagramming? Microsoft Visio.

These are merely examples, and there are other tools that can accomplish these tasks just as well. The key takeaway is that as a Business Analyst, you are expected to have a solid working knowledge of these tools on day 1 of a software development project.

What You Need to Know

I have yet to encounter a Business Analyst who is mediocre at using the Microsoft Office Suite of tools for documentation purposes, and if you are that unusual mediocre one, you can easily skill up in a few hours. A good way to, for example, upskill your Microsoft Office Suite skills is to review past documentation (if you can find it) and build on it.

You may feel like a bozo lost in the Word, Excel, PowerPoint, and Visio maze, but proficiency in this must-have skill is also the easiest to improve. There is a wealth of online resources that can be used to learn documentation skills, and depending on what needs to be learned, it can take anywhere from a few hours to a few days.

Software Development Methodologies Knowledge

While this is not a skill per se, it is important to know the differences between the major software development methodologies (Waterfall vs. Agile) as well as understand how they work. The mechanics of these software development have been explored in Chapter 2. As detailed in Chapter 2, a Business Analyst ought to know what software development methodologies are and more specifically the differences between Waterfall and Agile.

What You Need to Know

The methodologies in use on a project have direct impacts on Business Analyst deliverables and overall project delivery. Grasping the methodologies is a low-level effort, and the more projects a Business Analyst accomplishes, the more they are exposed to the finer details of software development methodologies.

Software Development Life Cycle Knowledge

This concept is also detailed in Chapter 2 and uses a case study that illustrates how the Software Development Life Cycle works on a real project. It refers to Business Analysts' knowledge of the framework that governs the process of software development. Under this framework, the development of a software product goes through these phases or some variation of these phases: Analysis, Requirements Planning/Scoping, Product Design, Product Development, Testing, and Deployment (or Go Live/Product Launch).

What You Need to Know

This is an important concept that a Business Analyst should be familiar with. It's also a straightforward one to learn and understand. Understanding this concept is enhanced with every additional software product development project a Business Analyst undertakes.

Technical Writing Skills

Technical writing has diverse practical applications in wide-ranging fields from technology to medicine to manufacturing, and it's concerned with simplifying complexity.

The main purpose of technical writing is to convey technical concepts in a format that can be easily understood by consumers of the information. The format it takes usually depends on the presenter, the audience, and the material being presented. Ultimately, it's best to accompany technical writing with illustrations, charts, screenshots, or process flow diagrams.

Technical writing is very useful during requirements scoping for it is important to communicate the desired outcomes *without* leaving gray areas, ambiguity, or confusion.

When a Business Analyst presents a requirement that is, for example, interpreted differently by different technical team members, then the technical writing has not effectively communicated the intention of the requirement. To be more specific, a software developer should review a requirement and be left in no doubt about the intention of that requirement.

Technical writing that clearly conveys the message in a communication gets everyone on the same page and saves a lot of time spent rewriting and clarifying that intent. Conversely, unclear technical writing creates holds up in the development life cycle as technical teams spend more time seeking clarifications. In extreme cases fuzzy technical writing can lead to the development of a product far removed from what end users asked for.

Business Analysts also need to be skilled technical writers when they draft end user instructional manuals as end users require this information in a writing style that they will easily understand

What You Need to Know

This is a learned skill, and there are bottomless resources on how to become an ace technical writer who delivers technical concepts using brevity, simplicity, and precision. Depending on the background of the Business Analyst, learning technical writing can be seamless, or it can take a while to become a well-polished skill. Business Analysts who have previously worked in sales/ business operations or worked with IT/technical teams seem to have the lowest barriers to learning technical writing, but anyone can still master technical writing by self-practice and referring to online resources.

Creating Use Cases

Use cases consider the scenarios or situations where a software product or application is used by end users. At their most basic level, use cases define a set of interactions between users and systems in a given setting.

"What is the business use case for this requirement?" is a frequently asked question during requirements scoping phases and requirements discovery sessions.

The intention of such a question is to check that the scenario being discussed is valid and has been experienced by the users who are requesting changes to a system, process, or software product.

Consider a discount approval process that requires three managerial approvals. To sales teams this is an unreasonable process, and as a use case, it demonstrates why the process needs to be shortened, maybe by removing one manager from this process.

What You Need to Know

Use cases are a powerful tool in understanding why change is needed, a must-have asset for any Business Analyst but also an easily learned and understood concept. There are many reference sources online that Business Analysts can use to upskill use case knowledge.

Analytical Skills

This falls in both the technical and non-technical skills areas—technical because a Business Analyst will analyze an end user problem and the data supporting it and either devise a solution or builds a case for a solution.

It may be non-technical analysis in that it involves scenario building and the likely impacts on users and processes then devising strategies for end user acceptance of the solution.

As a Business Analyst, you need analytical skills so that you can review an issue and methodically, logically, and creatively work toward a solution while noting the potential impacts of the solution. It may sound like simultaneously juggling many balls, but we do this all the time at work and in our personal lives. Analytical skills will be reviewed in Chapter 8 as part of Creativity and Problem-Solving Skills.

What You Need to Know

This is a skill that comes with experience, and after spending considerable time in the trade, using the analytical muscle becomes second nature.

Database Knowledge

Databases are an essential pillar of how software products and applications work, and it's important to have more than a passing knowledge of what they are and what they do.

In lay terms they are Excel like applications that store vast quantities of data points running into the millions. When an end user interacts with a software product or process by doing any type of data entry or data retrieval, just know there are many database functions going on in the background.

What You Need to Know

As a Business Analyst, you need to know the purpose and function of databases.

Most software development projects will at some point interface with changes to a database which could be data inputs, data retrieval, data storage, data analytics, and how different users access data. A few hours on Google will give you the critical knowledge you need for this key technical skill.

Data Analysis

Closely following on database knowledge is querying or searching the data inside databases using tools like SQL (Scripted Query Language). SQL queries extract data for export and consumption by end users like Business Analysts and other project team members. This is especially useful if you need to query large data sets to support business decisions or query datasets as part of software product testing.

Do you need to be a SQL expert to be an ace Business Analyst? Not at all.

While not all projects require SQL skills, some basic level of data querying knowledge is required as different software products on projects come equipped with reporting and analytics capabilities that can be used to query datasets.

To my mind it's more important to know where the data you need is located and how you will access it instead of brushing up SQL skills you will likely never use on a project. If you know how to run SQL queries, that's a great asset to have on a project especially if there is a need for it.

Conversely if you lack SQL skills and they are required on your project, you can acquire them in no time from a variety of online resources and public libraries. In general terms, even if you have zero SQL skills, there is no need to panic as depending on the project, you can still access and interpret data without running SQL queries.

Lately there are a number of powerful business analytics, dashboarding, and data visualization apps that not only help with generating large datasets but more importantly provide meaning and interpretation to those datasets. Data analysis is a wide discipline, and learning it takes some focus as well as dedicating a few hours for a couple of weeks to get a feel for how to use it depending on the requirement or the project.

What You Need to Know

Data analysis is a key component of the Software Development Life Cycle. Depending on the software product they are working with Business Analysts need to know how to access data for analysis and validation. What is important for this must-have skill is understanding how to access the data and its subsequent interpretation.

Process Mapping and Business Process Modeling

It is a general-purpose technique that visually illustrates a process flow, business workflow, or data flow. It can also be used to illustrate how different systems and process segments are related as well as how they deliver inputs or outputs to each other (see Figure 3-1). The main purpose of a process flow is to illustrate visually disparate process interconnections and relatedness.

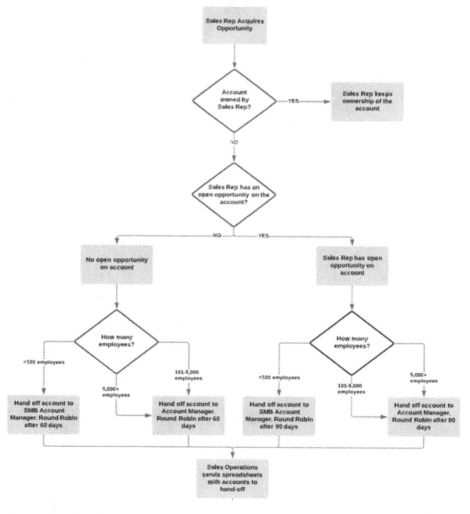

Figure 3-1. Sample Process Flow Diagram

Some requirements are best explained by showing project stakeholders a process map or diagram instead of verbalizing it. While the Microsoft Office Suite (especially Visio) is well equipped with process diagramming tools, there are many newer process mapping apps that are just as capable.

What You Need to Know

Process diagramming is a basic but essential tool in the Business Analyst toolkit for it puts the visual into the verbal and simplifies hitherto complex concepts. This is another easily learned technical skill that mostly requires practice to get a grip on it. There are also abundant online resources that provide instruction on learning and improving the use of process mapping.

Entity Relationship Diagrams (ERDs)

ERDs may look like process maps, but they are more focused on visually illustrating how the entities of an information system or data model are related to each other (See Figure 3-2). ERDs have their origins in the early phases of database development where they were developed for modeling databases.

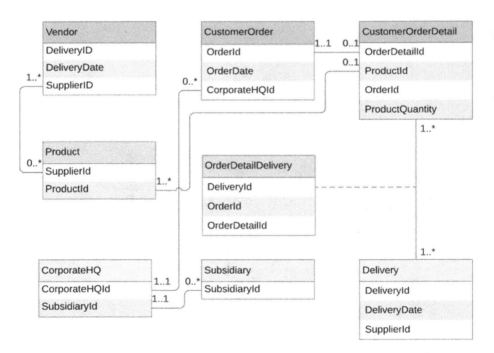

Figure 3-2. Sample Entity Relationship Diagram

While they are still used for data modeling, ERDs also have wider applications like illustrating information systems and the relationships between different entities and attributes. As an aside, ERDs use specific data modeling notations (for example 1..1 in the figure) that relay meaning to the different aspects of a data model or information system.

What You Need to Know

ERDs may not be easy on the eye at first glance, but users can become adept at using them if they repeatedly draft or interpret them. This is not a must-have technical skill, but you can be certain that at some point in your Business Analyst career, there will be a need to interpret an ERD diagram. Knowing when to use ERDs will put you in a good position when that time comes around. Just like process mapping, there are many online resources and publications that provide instruction on how to use ERDs.

Data Mapping

Data mapping is documentation that shows how data is mapped from one information system (or data model) to another information system (or data model) (Figure 3-3). You can take this advice to the bank: migrating and integrating data are processes that should never see the light of day *without* data mapping in place.

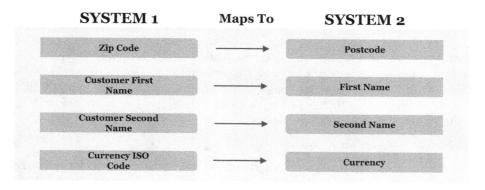

Figure 3-3. Sample Data Mapping Documentation

In its simplest form, data mapping is a guide that states how data points in an originating system are mapped to similar data points in another destination system.

It may for instance state that Point 3 in System A will send the data it collects to Point 3 in System X. In simple terms, if System A is shut down, the data will still be available in System X, and users can check Point 3 in System X to retrieve it.

This is a very vital component for data migrations. Mismatches or the lack of data mapping results in incorrect mappings that can severely compromise the quality of data in a data model or information system.

What You Need to Know

The first time I was asked to do data mapping, I went into a cold sweat for it was so intimidating and technically exotic. It turned out to be much easier than I thought. Don't let the term fool you; it's exactly what it is: data mapping between two information systems—an important skill that you will require if your project intends to work with data migrations and integrations.

Data mapping is mostly learned by doing, and in the event that a Business Analyst has zero data mapping knowledge, they can use online resources and data-related publications for upskilling which shouldn't take more than a few hours.

Product Testing

This covers basic knowledge about quality assurance (QA) and the role it plays in software product development. Business Analysts conduct product testing before formal User Acceptance Testing which is testing by end users or the eventual owners of the software product. As previously mentioned in Chapter 2, it is best practice for Business Analysts to test any product that has been given a clean bill of health by the development team before it is handed over to end users for testing.

What You Need to Know

Product testing is exactly what it means: you get to test whether a software product works as intended by the initial requirement. For Business Analysts the purpose of product testing is to validate that the delivered product meets the need that was requested by the requirement. This is a must-have skill that can be learned on day 1 of a software development project; it's that easy.

Wireframing and Prototyping

This refers to the "likeness" of a software product. As an example, it may be a sketch of a web application that shows the different web pages, or it may be a sketch of a web page that mimics a page on a web site. As with data analysis there are several prototyping apps that use color, content, and graphical elements to give a prototype or demo a richer life as well as a more realistic feel. Business Analysts with graphic design or photoshopping experience tend to shine when prototyping is required.

What You Need to Know

This is a great tool for demonstrating software product concepts to end users or audiences without information technology backgrounds. Prototyping is another skill that grows by practice, and learning it is largely dependent on the tool used by a Business Analyst as some tools are easier than others to use.

Project Management Skills

I have held both Business Analyst and Project Manager roles on the same project in a previous life, and it is important to understand that while the roles overlap, they are different. These are the instances when Business Analysts will occasionally wear the Project Manager's hat.

Managing Project Scope

What is going to be worked on (in scope) during a project and what will not be worked on (out of scope) are critical aspects of a Business Analysts' responsibilities. They ensure that the actual technical work *only* covers approved requirements. Any extra or unplanned end user requests (aka scope creep[1]) must be channeled through the normal requirements prioritization cycles.

While Project Managers govern project direction which includes project scope, Business Analysts work at the granular level to ensure that the scope is restricted to components and requirements that have been approved by project end users and stakeholders.

What You Need to Know

This is a must-have skill that cannot be built overnight but is honed over the years in the trenches of the Business Analyst trade. After a few projects, it starts to come effortlessly.

---

[1] Scope creep: the addition of extra requirements to be worked on when those requirements were not originally approved as part of the formal requirements scope of work.

Monitoring Project Timing

Managing project timing as an activity will usually not be assigned to a Business Analyst to oversee as that is the preserve of a Project Manager. However, project timelines are built on implicit assumptions that Business Analysts will deliver the inputs (requirements) required for a project to progress through the development cycle. If requirements are delayed or are not delivered at precisely the time they are required, then that project is unlikely to be delivered per agreed timelines. This is how Business Analyst deliverables impact project timelines.

What You Need to Know

As a Business Analyst, you must constantly watch timelines and how your deliverables impact those timelines. The key here is understanding the relationship between your deliverables and how they impact project timelines.

Project Budget Monitoring

Watching the pennies and dollars on a project is project managerial and project leadership territory. The project manager or the Project Management Office (PMO) resources the projects and monitors project spend periodically. However, it is not unheard of for projects to assign some form of budgetary monitoring responsibilities to Business Analysts. It may range from the simple stuff like reporting whether a project is red, yellow, or green in budgetary terms to the complex where Business Analysts need to monitor itemized spend and occasionally submit supplementary budget requests.

What You Need to Know

Monitoring budgets is not a must-do activity for Business Analysts; that is project manager or PMO territory. It is an unusual activity for Business Analysts but may be required depending on the project or organizational setup.

Project Team Management

Some project setups require Lead Business Analysts or Senior Business Analysts to manage projects, in lieu of a project manager. They will carry out project manager responsibilities as well as their functional Business Analyst roles.

What You Need to Know

Project management is not a must-have skill for Business Analysts. However, some projects require that their Business Analysts also lead projects, which means that a Business Analyst wearing this hat ought to be knowledgeable about general project management principles. Caught in this situation? Make use of online resources and available project management literature on how to manage software development projects.

Project Status Updates and Reporting

Business Analysts have to provide periodical status updates to project stakeholders for the duration of a project. An update could be as simple as a few lines of email stating recent updates or milestones completed. It could also be documentation that details among others achieved milestones, pending actions, next steps, blockers, risks, and overall project status (green, yellow, or red).

Some projects require that a Business Analyst provide their updates to a project manager who compiles updates from all project team members into one project status reporting document.

What You Need to Know

While project status reporting is not a must-have skill for Business Analysts, it is important that Business Analysts understand the role it plays during the project delivery process. The actual reporting content varies but expect reporting of some sort. Reporting has the added benefit of providing visibility to project progress, and as a Business Analyst, you should be worried if your project does not provide reporting or status updates.

Project Management Tools

The list of tools in use to run software development projects is never ending and continues to grow. The tools in use on a project largely come down to project leadership and their preferences for particular tools.

These tools are mainly concerned with tracking project progress and providing visibility to the different project components and work streams at any given point in time.

Some project tracking tools like Microsoft Project are used to track project progress, while other tools like JIRA are perfect for tracking individual requirements and where they are in the project cycle.

As an example, such a tool provides team members with visibility as to whether a requirement is in development or testing and whether it is blocked or waiting on another component for completion.

What You Need to Know

While tools like JIRA and its ilk sound complicated to use, they can be learned in a couple of hours. Not a must-have skill, but it helps if a Business Analyst understands what these tools are and what they do.

These are the critical skills that a Business Analyst will utilize in the process of software development project delivery. While each project has unique environments that may demand the deployment of certain technical skills that are not covered here, the above skills are what the majority of projects expect their Business Analysts to be equipped with and be knowledgeable about.

We now turn our attention to the optional technical skills and how Business Analysts can use them to build a well-rounded portfolio of technical skills.

Optional Technical Skills

Unlike the previous chapter that discussed must-have technical skills, this chapter will go over a few technical skills that are optional, but are good to have.

Domain Experience

Business Analysts can specialize in software products and technologies specific to industries like manufacturing or healthcare, and some Business Analyst positions require domain experience for a specific industry or technology. Some Business Analysts also specialize in specific technologies like database management or enterprise resource planning (ERP) systems.

What You Need to Know

Accumulating specific domain or technology experience gives you added insights and perspectives in a Business Analyst role specific to that domain. However, it's not a career wrecker should you find yourself working with a new technology or industry where you lack deep experience. This is a personal preference determined by the career choices of a Business Analyst. Gaining domain knowledge comes from placements on projects in that particular domain that a Business Analyst has chosen to specialize in, and the more projects that are accomplished, the more domain expertise a Business Analyst acquires.

© Roni Lubwama 2020
R. Lubwama, *The Inside Track to Excelling As a Business Analyst*,
https://doi.org/10.1007/978-1-4842-5543-8_4

Six Sigma and Lean Management

These are entire management disciplines by themselves, and at their core, they are management techniques used to significantly improve quality and process management using statistical modeling methods in organizations. At a high level, these management principles are used to make organizational processes more efficient and effective. Organizations that are wedded to these disciplines usually require Six Sigma–certified Business Analysts so that they can deploy these techniques to drive organizational changes.

What You Need to Know

Organizations on a Six Sigma or Lean Management high usually mean it and will only work with Business Analysts who understand and have experience with these management disciplines. In short, you either have this expertise or you don't. If this is the requirement to work on their projects, then you need to skill up. Fast.

For Business Analysts who want to work on projects that require this knowledge or for those who find themselves on a project with this requirement, there are many resources they can fall back on for knowledge acquisition and certification.

These management disciplines have been around for a while, and there are many institutions that offer training for them. In addition, there are numerous online courses, publications, as well as many more books that have been written about Six Sigma or Lean Management.

Web Services and Web Development

Most organizational digital transformations will involve web services and web development components. Web services is how different applications communicate with each other over the Internet, while web development refers to the development of web sites, web portals, web apps, and associated applications. The requirements scoped by Business Analysts will usually deliver elements of web services and web applications–related software as their end products.

What You Need to Know

While it is helpful for a Business Analyst to understand this functionality (it helps with requirements scoping), it is not essential to, for example, know concepts like the configuration of a web service call.

Application Configuration

I am hard-pressed classifying this as a "nice to have" technical skill as it is becoming more frequent for Business Analyst roles requiring some basic application configuration. In simple terms, application configuration refers to using the settings in a software application to make changes to the application so that end users can deliver different outputs from the application. Another way to look at it is when changes are made to an application without the modification of that application's code or writing new programs and inserting them in the application.

This is a skill that is primarily determined by project requirements and organizational objectives. Depending on the type of Business Analyst role, some organizations require that a Business Analyst demonstrate knowledge of how to configure an application. Whether you need this skill or not comes down to the project you are assigned to and whether the organization you work for requires configuration skills for the role.

What You Need to Know

While application configuration is not a key requirement, the best Business Analysts usually have some configuration knowledge, and they tend to know how and when to use it. Fortunately, it is also easily learned as the more time spent inside an application, the more polished configuration skills become. Configuration skills are also driven by the application that a Business Analyst works with on a project as some applications are easily configurable and some require more technical expertise in order to configure them.

In terms of knowledge acquisition, there are thousands of online courses and professional certifications that provide instruction on how to configure any application under the sun in a matter of hours.

Programming Languages

Some Business Analysts having transitioned from software development environments understand one or more programming languages like Java, JavaScript, Python, and many more. Most Business Analysts will never write a line of code during their career, and I would tread very carefully if I am asked to write code as a Business Analyst given the technical competencies and skillsets it requires. A Business Analyst with programming experience can, for example, troubleshoot bugs and defects which hastens the defect management process, but then again that is not the essence of having Business Analysts on project teams. There are developers and quality assurance engineers on projects for precisely this reason.

What You Need to Know

If you have experience with programming languages, count that as an uber luxury for your Business Analyst technical skillset. Conversely if you lack this experience or skillset, there is no need to be anguished as you don't need programming skills to be an ace Business Analyst.

Technical Certifications

There are certifications offered by the International Institute of Business Analysis (IIBA) which certify that a Business Analyst has acquired the experience and professional training required to become a business analysis practitioner.

There are also certifications native to different enterprise applications that offer professional training on end user functionality, configuration, and even customization.

Acquiring certifications as a Business Analyst gives you deeper insights into how these applications or disciplines (in the case of business analysis or Agile certifications) function or operate. They are not must-have's unless you are in a Business Analyst role where they are a key requirement. In general terms acquiring certifications is a recommended career path if you intend to stay in the Business Analyst role for the long term.

What You Need to Know

Certifications are not must-have's required by Business Analysts unless you are assigned to a project where it's a key requirement for the role. While they signify expertise and professional competence in a given field, their absence in your skillset as a Business Analyst is not a deal breaker, and you can still deliver outstanding results without them especially if you have many years of experience.

This list of technical skills is by no means exhaustive, but these are the usual suspects when it comes to the technical skills expected to be deployed by Business Analysts. If you are wondering what determines the application of certain skills and not others on a project, that determination is usually driven by organizational cultures and project setups.

Nevertheless, there are some key technical skills that a Business Analyst is expected to have on day 1 on a project assignment. Does this mean you are useless without these skills? Of course not. If you find yourself in the unenviable position of running a project that requires these skills, you can quickly acquire these skills through self-study, practice, mentoring, or observation. In any case if you managed to get the Business Analyst role in the first place, then skilling up should not be an issue.

But there are skills that are not easily switched on and for which skilling up comes with hands-on experience and much more; to those skills we turn to next.

Importance of Non-technical Skillsets

Gone are the days when a Business Analyst could largely deliver a project by relying mostly on technical skills such as data analysis. Back then, Business Analysts could layer technical skills with communication skills and stakeholder management, for example, and be able to deliver digital transformation projects successfully.

Times have changed so drastically that these approaches that were deployed successfully two decades ago are not enough to pass muster today as Business Analysts are held to a far higher standard of project delivery and execution. This is what has changed in the intervening period:

- Digital transformation projects are now more complex and far-reaching in their scope and impacts.

- Project failure does not stop at financial losses; it translates into lost opportunities, diminished corporate profiles, and shredded personal reputations among other downsides. In a roundabout way, the costs of project failure or the delivery of sub-par projects are very high.

© Roni Lubwama 2020
R. Lubwama, *The Inside Track to Excelling As a Business Analyst*,
https://doi.org/10.1007/978-1-4842-5543-8_5

- Technology evolves very rapidly with the effect that one misstep can prove very costly in terms of innovation, future technology transitions, and the effort required to catch up in technological terms.

Depending on the demands of the project the Business Analyst is assigned to or the organization that employs them, they can deploy a wide range of non-technical skills to deliver project objectives

These skills range from communication skills to interpersonal skills to problem-solving skills, and they can be deployed by Business Analysts depending on the need or challenges in front of them. The subsequent chapters cover these skills as well as other improvised work-arounds that can be used during the process of project delivery.

Additionally, Business Analysts need to bring a touch of non-technical skills to the tools they mainly use for project execution and delivery. There are best practices, for example, on how Business Analysts can make the most of email communications and meetings/presentations so that they can efficiently and effectively deliver their projects. These too will be considered in this chapter.

But first, let's consider some challenges particular to the Business Analyst practice that require the use of non-technical skills and subsequently how these skills can be used to overcome those challenges.

Challenges of the Business Analyst Role

The challenges discussed in this section demonstrate why Business Analysts need a wide and deep repertoire of non-technical skills during the process of project delivery.

Lack of Enforcement Abilities

While there is a lot expected from Business Analysts, they unfortunately have very little authority, enforcement abilities, or coercive powers to achieve these objectives. Business Analysts are rarely (if ever) given the authority to fire or sanction project team members or any other project actors. The closest they can get is to recommend the removal of a disruptive team member from a project, but even that recommendation is not guaranteed to be carried out. In fact, if Business Analysts wanted, they could harangue, scream, bully, or cajole project team members and stakeholders to do what they want and still *never* get anything done. In the absence of coercive powers, they have to rely on *soft powers* which are really non-technical skills to deliver what is expected of them.

Changing Mind-Sets and Attitudes

Business Analysts are in the business of changing minds, changing work routines, and facilitating organizational change. Human beings are creatures of habit as well as routine, and we resist change because we are comfortable with what we know or what works best for us regardless of efficiency. It would seem counterintuitive, but change is not always welcomed by some end users, stakeholders, and other project actors with a vested interest in project outcomes.

Peculiarities of the Business Analyst Practice

There is a special emphasis on non-technical skills in the Business Analyst practice because the role has unique project and people management challenges that come to the fore during the project delivery process. These challenges cannot be resolved by technical abilities alone; rather they are defused by cleverly deploying non-technical skills and layering the appropriate technical skills. While each project has a set of challenges particular to it, there is a category of challenges that are the usual staple on most projects. Some of those challenges are highlighted here.

1. Resistance to Change

Change Means New Mind-Sets and New Ways of Working

Let's assume you have been using Excel for the last couple of years for data entry and analysis. You have souped up your spreadsheets with fancy macros and all manner of formulas, and these spreadsheets have worked great for you in that time. But there is a problem with this setup; the knowledge inherent in this setup and the use of this process are localized only to you, and few people know what you do or how you do it. If you left the organization today, that knowledge walks out the door with you.

In the interests of efficiency and collaboration, organizational management has decided to move to a cloud-based application which means your fancy spreadsheets are getting the axe and you will need to be trained to use the new application. Would you be happy about these changes? That depends on why you show up to work every day.

Some folks will be outrightly hostile and will want to continue using their spreadsheets instead of the new application. Other end users may be indifferent, and some will immediately sign on to the proposal as they have always wanted a better tool. The holdouts above and the need to gain acceptance to across the board changes are the main reasons why software project delivery is so challenging. Accepting change is going to be difficult because it involves changing mind-sets to new technologies and the removal of entrenched but inefficient ways of working.

A Business Analyst working on such initiatives can use non-technical skills to bring in the holdouts resistant to the proposed changes.

Change Requires Retraining and Learning

Business and process changes usually require learning new processes or how new applications work. End users need to become adept at learning new technologies and how to navigate new applications. While it may look like simply learning new web page navigations, not all end users will embrace the need to relearn, and they will resist the changes. This situation is made more complex if the holdouts are also the end users who are meant to be the technology or application evangelists.

Change Brings Transparency, Visibility, Accountability, and Efficiency

Depending on the reasons for implementing change and if the project is successfully delivered, an organization can break cycles of nonperformance and see efficiency and productivity gains. This does not mean all end users will be thrilled to see nonperformance get the axe. Some end users thrive in unstructured environments that lack transparency and visibility to how they work. This category of users is certain to resist business and process changes that bring them into the open where there is more accountability and transparency.

2. Scope Creep and Fluid Expectations

When a project is in motion and end users keep insisting on adding new requirements that were not part of the initial approved requirements or scope, then you get scope creep. Sometimes for reasons well beyond them, end users keep changing what they want the final product to look like or what it will do.

It may be that they no longer have the budget to deliver the project as intended, or it could be that they work with very rapidly changing market conditions and must respond to market pressures or get caught by competitors. Of course, these frequent scope changes are going to cause a fair amount of eye-rolling by project team members who resent being in such a state of flux.

These types of situations are checked and managed by the use of non-technical skills.

3. Office Politics

Where you have humans clustered together working to achieve an objective, you will have politics of some sort; it's been that way since we left the jungles. Project environments are no different, and they will be buffeted by office politics as well. Having stated that fact, consider two ways in which office politics can hamper project delivery:

- **Irregular Flow of Communication**

  Important information does not reach all team members, and stakeholders withhold critical information from some project members. This leads to different team members working at cross purposes because they are outside the information loop

- **Management by Cliques**

  Because organizational or project leadership indirectly manages the organization by encouraging cliques, different people are allied to different objectives far removed from project objectives. There is no unity of purpose due to project team members, end users, and stakeholders working in cliques or factions.

Business Analysts need to deploy non-technical skills to mitigate the corrosive impacts of office politics on project delivery and execution.

4. Disruptive Stakeholder Agendas

These are the individuals or entities that have a vested interest in the successful outcomes of a project. They may be end users and their managers, project team members, executive leadership, other departments, other business organizations, or even external entities like vendors.

While stakeholders can be counted on to provide project support, leadership, and governance, sometimes their agendas run counter to what a project seeks to achieve. In effect, they present the kind of situations where Business Analysts must use non-technical skills to align project and stakeholder objectives. It's a good idea to review how this misalignment is manifested.

Stakeholder Pet Projects (Real vs. Perceived Needs)

A stakeholder is interested in a project that brings no real value to a business or process, or they stymie a project with real and quantifiable benefits to the same business or process. They resist collaboration on a project because their "pet project" is not in the running. Alternatively, they can "slow walk" project progress because they did not generate, lead, or champion the project.

Project Wreckers

A stakeholder technically wrecks a project by not providing support, documentation, and end users for requirements elicitation. They may, for example, request functionality that they know cannot be delivered and insist on launching the product with that functionality. These actions are usually a smokescreen for subterfuge. The real reasons could be fear of a loss of influence, loss of budgetary clout, loss of corporate/department stature, or perceived demotion due to the implementation of new processes.

Sometimes a project stakeholder is interested in seeing a project stalled due to their ego being rubbed the wrong way. They are perceived as the leaders in the organization, and they want their name stamped on anything of significance in the organization. They therefore feel slighted and walked over when a project is initiated and delivered without their input or stamp of approval. They may not want to completely fail the project, but they "slow walk" it until the project team becomes deferential to them or strokes their ego in order to get their cooperation.

This scenario also includes intransigent project team members who insist on doing things their way, which hinders project teamwork and collaboration.

Dealing with project wreckers and getting them to cooperate is probably one of the toughest aspects of the Business Analyst practice, and as you may have guessed, these are situations tailor-made for resolution by non-technical skills.

Lack of Ownership and Accountability

Consider a situation where the Business Requirement Document is ready for sign off, but no one is willing to sign it off. The Business Analyst chases signatures, but none are forthcoming, and the situation has the air of a lack of responsibility and accountability. End users or stakeholders do not want to put pen to paper, which could be due to any or all the following reasons:

- They don't expect the process changes to be a success, and they don't want to be associated with the subsequent flop not to mention the repercussions arising from the said flop.

- Everyone is waiting for someone else to sign off.

- They don't want to get flamed by their managers when they issue the sign offs.

- They are waiting for someone senior or above them to sign off.

- They do not have the actual authority to sign off.

- They don't know what they are signing off, so they would rather not sign off at all.

Withholding Information and Documentation

If an influential end user or stakeholder is resistant to change, guess what they are going to do? "Slow walk" the delivery of information needed for requirements scoping. They could also stump efforts to deliver process documentation and Subject Matter Experts that are needed for requirements elicitation.

Obviously without information, documentation, or input from Subject Matter Experts, a Business Analyst cannot do much by way of requirements scoping which was the intention of the "slow walkers" in the first place.

The Business Analyst is ready to drive someplace, but the tires have been slashed.

This challenge is impervious to resolution by technical skills alone and is in a way a logical conclusion of issues 1–4 and the most commonly used vehicle by "slow walkers" to drive their misguided points home.

Ace Business Analysts who have encountered these situations before are well primed with the appropriate non-technical skills that will resolve the bottlenecks in front of them.

This chapter has been a consideration of why Business Analysts need non-technical skills during the project delivery process. We now turn to a review of these non-technical skills individually and how Business Analysts utilize them to deliver projects as well as resolving project delivery challenges.

Communication Skills

There are not many subjects in business literature that have been written about as much as communication skills. Given that there is a wealth of knowledge about communication skills, it's easy to assume that everyone "gets" how to communicate or that they understand the impacts of poor communication skills. Unfortunately, this is not the case given the projects that flounder due to poor communications skills.

Given that the Business Analyst role is an important cog in the software product development process, the expectation is that the person holding this role should be an excellent communicator. This is because this role acts as an orchestrator heavily reliant on a diverse set of communication skills that ensure that key actors remain connected and in continuous motion toward the product envisioned by end users and stakeholders.

A few scenarios that require deft communication skills come to mind:

- **Requirements Scoping**

    Business Analysts need to elicit requirements from end users and stakeholders. This is a need that is fulfilled by clearly verbalizing and visualizing information to end users to confirm what their requirements are. This runs the gamut from eliciting simple minute details to the major product components.

© Roni Lubwama 2020
R. Lubwama, *The Inside Track to Excelling As a Business Analyst*,
https://doi.org/10.1007/978-1-4842-5543-8_6

- **Interactions with Technical Teams**

  Business Analysts interact heavily with technical teams, and they need to be able to relay end user requirements in a way that removes any ambiguity and gray areas.

- **Interactions with Project Stakeholders**

  Business Analysts are in constant communication with project team members, end users, and stakeholders about project progress, assignments, milestones, blockers, and dependencies. None of these can be delivered without finely honed communication skills.

Situations Requiring Top-Notch Communication Skills

There will be times when Business Analysts need to persuade, cajole, influence, or negotiate with stakeholders, project team members, and other parties vested in the delivery of the end user product. These are typical scenarios for which top-notch communication skills are required.

For Business Analysts to deliver these assignments, they need to deploy a diverse set of communication skills that encompass personal communication skillsets as well as the skillful use of productivity tools (e.g., email) that foster communication.

Regardless of Business Analyst communication abilities or how they harness productivity tools, the result should be information that is delivered with clarity and conciseness as well as information that eliminates guess work and removes gray areas.

Key Communication Skills

There are many types of communication skills, but for our purposes, we will consider seven key communication skills that enable Business Analysts to excel at their craft. These are also the communication modes that Business Analysts rely on multiple times on any given day and utilize the most during the process of project delivery.

- **Verbal Skills**

  This refers to talking to and speaking with an audience in a style, language, and tone that effectively delivers information. This can be delivered to an audience of one or many people.

- **Documentation Skills**

  This skill has been partially detailed in Chapter 3 as it has one foot in technical writing, and it refers to understanding how to convey information in technical terms when sharing a document or sending an email, for example. Even more important is knowing when to dump the techy jargon depending on the audience that will receive the documentation being circulated.

- **Active Listening**

  This refers not to merely listening as another person is speaking but being engaged with the message, processing the information as it is being heard, and confirming the content with the speaker.

- **Body Language**

  This is in reference to interpreting not only what is spoken but also the nonverbal cues that accompany the verbalized message in order to get a fuller picture of the content that is delivered.

- **Managing Email Communications**

  Business Analysts spend a lot of time managing email (sending, receiving, replying, and composing emails) and it is logical that there is an understanding of how to use this tool effectively and efficiently.

- **Meeting, Presentation, and Facilitation Skills**

  This is another mode of communication that gobbles up an inordinate amount of a Business Analyst's time. Understanding how to make the most of meetings and presentations inevitably results in more efficient Business Analysts and effective delivery of information.

- **Tact and Diplomacy Skills**

  This is the ability to review a situation or setting and know when to say something, how to say it, and more importantly, know what to say.

Mastering the aforementioned communication skills enables Business Analysts to consistently deliver their projects. Additionally, the skills do not exist or work in isolation; they are dependent on each other as well as other skills like interpersonal skills. Active listening for instance goes hand in glove with speaking and presentation skills. Being an active listener who cannot command an audience during meetings is not very effective in the long run either.

Different Business Analysts have different strengths and weaknesses when it comes to the communication skillset, but strengthening each one of them will eventually improve their overall communication skillset.

The Importance of Communication Skills

There are downsides to Business Analysts being sloppy in the management of communication tools or being personally mediocre at communications in a project setting, and here's how.

Inability to Seal the Deal

How does a Business Analyst seal the deal without finessing a diverse set of communication skills? Consider a high-level executive who is also the project sponsor who won't sign off a requirements document. What is a Business Analyst to do? They will use a combination of presentation, negotiation, and communication skills to convince the stakeholder to provide the sign off they need to proceed with project delivery. This sounds obvious, but it isn't, and it's a reminder of the importance of mastering communication skills in a project setting.

The wider point though is that in the Business Analyst practice, successfully closing negotiations and changing minds are going to be very challenging without excellent communication skills.

Compromised Product Delivery

There is a very real risk of developing a product at odds with end user requirements if there is a communication lapse in the product development process. It is for this reason that Business Analysts need to master the art of clearly communicating requirements to technical teams and ensuring that any blind spots or areas of confusion are clarified. Similarly, they need to convey with clarity to end users the product they will be receiving and eliminate surprises later in the project cycle.

Information Gaps

A lack of adequate communication creates not only a risk of compromised products but also information gaps that can imperil the product development process. This is manifested in information either not flowing upward or downward on a project team. Team members caught in this information exclusion zone are always playing catch up and will at some point miss critical project milestones and deadlines.

Foments Conflicts

Business Analysts usually resolve conflicts between project team members as well as stakeholders. Resolving these tensions and conflicts aids the forward motion of projects, while projects mired in perpetual conflicts make the work of successful project delivery very difficult.

As an example, a Business Analyst whose verbal communication is abrasive, insensitive, and aggressive creates unnecessary conflicts that divert precious time and resources to resolve. These conflicts also degrade the professionalism and credibility of the Business Analyst.

Additionally, a Business Analyst that lacks finesse in deftly communicating with different audiences will not only fail to build relationships but is likely to break existing ones.

Rework (And a Lot of It)

Anytime an audience repeatedly asks for clarifications on the same subject during a communication event or post the communication event, then the communication is lacking in clarity or conciseness.

This leads to more meetings, more presentations, and more emails all seeking to clarify what was initially discussed. This is rework, and all it does is take time away from other more pressing project activities. There is also the opportunity cost incurred in the engaging of repeat work as opposed to pursuing activities that are more productive to project progress.

Credibility

One way to quickly and effectively trash a reputation or one's credibility is to hold meetings, speak to audiences, or generally communicate in a state of unpreparedness. This is manifested in a lack of background research, disjointed presentations, inaccurate facts, and grammatical errors. A general lack of preparedness blocks critical content from getting through to the audience as well as preventing a healthy dialogue from taking place. It also conveys a lack of professionalism from the speaker or presenter, and don't be surprised if some in the audience question the speaker or presenter's competence for the task, not to mention that sloppiness of the presenter distracts from the content that needs to be discussed.

Verbal Communication Skills

During the life span of a project, Business Analysts are going to speak to a wide range of audiences, from one person meetings to meetings with many end users and stakeholders. Holding the attention of their audience and ensuring that the other party understands what the Business Analyst is saying are a must-have skill.

Here's why the spoken word reigns supreme in communication skills:

- **Relaying Information**

    Business Analysts must convey end user requirements to technical teams in a format, style, and language that technical teams can understand. They also need to convey the same technical concepts to end users and stakeholders in a format they can easily understand.

- **Relationship and Rapport Building**

    Whether it is a one-on-one meeting in a hallway or a group meeting, speaking with focus, respect, and confidence builds relationships and helps builds rapport with end users, stakeholders, and project team members alike.

    Conversely speaking patronizingly or condescendingly will not endear a Business Analyst to the audiences they need to cultivate close relationships with. Business Analysts who master this skill get even the most difficult stakeholders to assent to their requests.

- **Demonstrates Conviction and Credibility**

    Conveying a message or trying to persuade someone in person is very different from doing it while "hidden" behind the digitally walled-off enclosure that is Microsoft Outlook. A phone conversation has the same effect for the other party cannot see a Business Analyst grimace or roll their eyes when they say something the Business Analyst considers particularly irritating.

    In-person meetings remove those protections (if you can call them that). In-person meetings exude confidence and the courage of one's convictions which conveys the message that the Business Analyst is confident about the content they are delivering and that they want the audience on their side.

Well, what about distributed teams that lack the ability to just walk down the hallway to resolve an issue with a team member? There's web calls and livestreamed video calling for that, and the principles that hold true for conducting in-person meetings hold true for the virtual world as well.

How Can Business Analysts Improve This Skill?

Match the Language to the Audience

Business Analysts must be mindful of the audience and tailor the language, jargon, and vocabulary accordingly. Depending on whether the audiences consists of end users, stakeholders, or project team members, Business Analysts must be mindful of the language, jargon, and style of presentation if they are going to get their message through. Talk in technical terms, and they stand to lose end users and stakeholders; if they cannot clearly elaborate the requirement or use case, then they lose project team members.

For discussions mired in disagreements, lack of clarity or ambiguity, visual aids like process maps or prototypes can be used to close information gaps and break the deadlock.

Build Content Knowledge

While it's not a requirement to have full mastery of the content under discussion, it certainly helps if Business Analysts do their homework as well as anticipate likely points of contention. This research helps Business Analysts ably deliver information without getting sidetracked by obvious knowledge gaps.

Build Confidence Through Preparation

Confidence is usually a by-product of research, for research enables Business Analysts to speak confidently about the subject matter at hand.

Be Mindful of Body Language

Match delivery of the spoken word with corresponding nonverbal cues. This would include actions like making eye contact with the audience, standing upright, and avoiding fidgeting with items like pens or devices during a presentation.

Resist the Hard Sell

There is a temptation to put pressure on the other party to accept or sign off without delay what is under discussion.

Consider a situation where a Business Analyst seeks a requirements approval from an end user during a meeting. This is called the hard sell, the type you experience when a used car salesman tries to sell you a lemon. This is usually counterproductive, and what works best is giving the end users and stakeholders time to evaluate the concepts that have just been discussed. There are other ways to get what the Business Analyst needs without using hard sell tactics.

Documentation and Writing Skills

Business Analysts draft and circulate documents like requirements documents, meeting minutes, emails, project status updates, as well as updating information on shared documentation websites, intranet web sites or wikis.

Business analysts need documentation and writing skills because the documents they draft and subsequently share are essentially documents of record. They can be referred to any time by either the sender or the recipient. With this in mind, a Business Analyst needs to ensure that any document they author and circulate is well-written, structured properly, and has good grammar. Anything less creates more rework by providing more explanations and context. A Business Analyst ought to ensure that not only are they proud of their output before they hit "Send" or "Enter" but that they can defend and speak intelligently about the content in the document.

How Can Business Analysts Improve This Skill?

Match the Language to the Audience

Business Analysts must understand when to use and when not to use techy jargon; it does not work for all audiences. Who are they sending a document to? Is it a project sponsor, end users, or developers? They need to keep in mind who is receiving their documentation and tailor it accordingly. Another thing to consider is that some audiences prefer visualized information like charts, process maps, or diagrams instead of text or verbal explanations. If a Business Analyst is having a difficult time getting content through to their audience by verbalizing it, then visualizing it is a better option.

Relevant Content and Good Grammar

Long winding documents with badly constructed sentences will garner few active readers. Brevity, shorter sentences, good grammar, simple vocabulary, relevant content, and well-structured paragraphs all make for better reading.

Active Listening

We all have different modes of listening when we are spoken to, and those modes determine if we fully capture what we are listening to especially the important points.

This is the VVIP of skills for Business Analysts (if there is such a thing) as a lack of active listening can lead to the building of false assumptions with the downstream effect of delivering an incomplete or wrong product.

Active listening refers to understanding, mentally evaluating what is being said in real time, and confirming with the speaker what a listener has just heard. It allows Business Analysts to think through what is being said and ask for confirmations or elicit more information from the speaker in real time so that they are clear about what they have just heard.

Here's why active listening is an essential skill in the Business Analyst toolkit:

- **Access to Information**

    It may sound obvious, but how else does a Business Analyst gain access to information and evaluate it without listening? How does a Business Analyst change minds without listening to the concerns of the audience? Better still, how does a Business Analyst compose intelligent responses to questions if they are not listening to their audiences?

- **Provides Clarity**

    Listening provides the opportunity to remove or clarify false assumptions while affirming correct assumptions. It also provides clarity where there are gray areas or points of confusion, and it helps filter the important from the trivial.

- **Builds Credibility and Trust**

    Listening to stakeholders and project team members even when Business Analysts disagree with their opinions builds credibility and trust, which are essential ingredients for collaboration on projects. Stakeholders can be difficult to deal with especially when they feel that they are not being listened to or that their opinions don't matter. They may have the dumbest ideas, but they still need to air them and be given audience by Business Analysts.

How Can Business Analysts Improve This Skill?

Paying Attention to the Speaker

Business Analysts ought to give the person speaking to them their full attention. When being spoken to, Business Analysts also need to keep interruptions and distractions to a minimum given that they are processing the information as they are hearing it.

Staying Engaged

By staying engaged with the discussion, Business Analysts can catch faulty assumptions, logic, flawed arguments or data, and other such inconsistencies. This cannot happen without physically and mentally engaging with the discussion in real time. Paraphrasing questions is a good way to get confirmation and clarification from a speaker if they are following a line of argument that is unclear. Statements like "do I have this right" or "this is what I am hearing, please confirm..." are perfect when clarity is required by a Business Analyst from an end user or stakeholder.

Staying Open Minded

As a meeting attendee, I will be quick to mentally squelch the ideas being presented as impractical which immediately closes my mind to the possibility that the ideas can work. It's best to keep an open mind and listen to what is being said in the moment; passing judgement on practicality can always come later.

Following up on the above, Business Analysts need to bring an attitude of "I don't know everything" to listening sessions. When they listen with the attitude "I know this stuff, so I don't need to listen," they miss out on what the wider conversation has to offer other than just that one part of the conversation they heard.

Additionally, the speaker will notice via nonverbal cues that the Business Analyst is not tuned in to their presentation which could be seen as being disrespectful or a lack of interest in the discussion.

It's Not Personal

On projects there will be moments when the presentation or ideas of a Business Analyst come under such intense scrutiny that it may feel like they are personally being questioned or attacked. There is a temptation to take it personally and to counter the questioning with aggressive tactics of their own like glaring at the audience or making snarky and sarcastic responses.

This is counterproductive as it's very likely that the stakeholders will respond in kind or they will remind the Business Analyst of this response at a most inconvenient time in the future.

In this business, Business Analysts must check their egos at the door and respond intelligently to the critiques they are hearing. It's difficult, but they must resist the temptation to take it personally simply because a person is giving them a hard time with their irritating questions.

Being warm and effusive and listening actively will likely disarm the most aggressive stakeholder in the room and deliver the objectives of the meeting than if the Business Analyst countered with intimidating tactics of their own.

Practice and More Practice

It comes down to practice. If Business Analysts are not inclined to actively listen, then this skill will take a while to mature. But after they have been burned by not listening actively, they will be more than ready the next time such a situation comes around. Practice; watch and practice some more is the name of the game.

Body Language

You have probably heard the saying, "it isn't what you say, it is *how* you say it." This is the essence of body language and communication by way of nonverbal cues.

In general terms body language refers to the use of physical bodily postures or positions to convey messages and communication. Along with posturing it also requires being mindful of the unspoken, turns of phrases, double meanings, and listening for what is unsaid sometimes deliberately.

Clearly there are many ways Business Analysts can use positive and negative body language or nonverbal cues to communicate with project team members or stakeholders.

Even allowing for cultural differences that carry different interpretations for different nonverbal cues, there are generally accepted interpretations of some nonverbal cues that Business Analysts should keep in mind when they interact with project team members, end users, and stakeholders.

For instance, sitting forward or making eye contact is considered positive body language and being receptive to the speaker. Negative body language can consist of zero eye contact or a folded arms posture which may indicate discomfort or lack of interest in what is being said.

The Importance of Body Language and Non-Verbal Cues

Here is how understanding the use of body language and nonverbal cues as a Business Analyst is of critical importance.

- **Managing In-Person Meetings**

  Is the person Business Analysts speaking to distracted? Are their thoughts elsewhere? Are they fidgeting with pens or looking out the window or the dead giveaway: checking their watch? These are signs that this is a meeting that needs to be timed out or rescheduled. Insisting on seeing this meeting through in the same format will not deliver the objectives it was scheduled for. This fidgety person is obviously disinterested in what the Business Analyst has to say; they are just not saying it out loud.

  Looking out for these nonverbal cues like when a stakeholder reluctantly agrees to something when their body language says otherwise saves a lot of time and expensive surprises later in the project cycle.

  I have experienced this scenario firsthand having been in meetings with a manager who was always distracted by phone calls, text messages, and flights he had to catch. To say that the meetings were unproductive is to put it mildly.

  To wiggle out of this meeting diplomatically, I politely inquired if he could provide me with an end user we could use for requirements scoping which he agreed to. This arrangement (which worked spectacularly) saved me the trouble of eliciting requirements from a stakeholder who clearly had more important things on his mind than discussing requirements for their project.

- **Managing Group Meetings and Presentations**

  A Business Analyst in a requirement review meeting with end users, and stakeholders ought to monitor the mood and interest levels of the audience if they want to get maximum value from a meeting.

  Is the audience sitting upright or slouched? Are they nodding off or alert? Are they having side conversations or focused on the presenter? Are they checking mail and doing mundane activities on their devices?

These are cues for an audience that has tuned out the Business Analyst doing the presentation. The Business Analyst needs to switch gears and figure out a way to be more engaging by not just droning on but having a conversation instead of a sermon.

Is the audience fatigued? Maybe the meetings should be shorter and held earlier in the day. Devices creating distractions? Make the meetings short, engaging, and lay out ground rules at the beginning of the meeting about the use of devices during the presentation.

Keeping a tab on nonverbal cues in group meetings and making subtle changes will ensure that a Business Analyst achieves the objectives of holding the presentation or meeting.

• Managing Business Analyst Presentations

It's fine considering nonverbal cues from a group audience or meeting partner, but how about nonverbal cues from the Business Analyst delivering the presentation or driving the meeting?

Are they making eye contact? Is their voice low, or are they mumbling their words? Do they look like they are rushing through the meeting so they can be somewhere else?

Body language and nonverbal cues cut two ways; they are essential for both Business Analysts and their audiences. It's obvious when a Business Analyst is distracted and is not fully "into" their own presentation: it shows in their body language (minimal eye contact, mumbled words and explanations that don't add up).

Sometimes they are just having a bad day and the presentation comes off as disjointed or lacking in preparation; presentation slides are missing, or they are using information from the last project (typical copy and paste).

These situations carry far graver implications for Business Analysts as the audience or meeting partners can also catch onto these cues and shut out the Business Analyst. They reason that if the Business Analyst is that disinterested in their own presentation or meeting, why should they as stakeholders be interested?

Does this mean that the Business Analyst should spend their waking hours on the hunt for nonverbal cues from everyone they work with on a project? That wouldn't be practical, but they need to be adept at reading the moods of their audiences and, if necessary, switch gears so that the objectives of the meeting or presentation are met.

While some degree of caution is required in the interpretation of nonverbal cues as sometimes there is not much to interpret, it would be foolhardy to ignore nonverbal cues altogether.

How Can Business Analysts Improve This Skill?

Gaining Experience

The more interactions Business Analysts have with stakeholders and project members, the more they become adept at reading nonverbal cues and interpreting body language signals. This skill grows with time and the more projects a Business Analyst undertakes.

Review Body Language Literature

There are so many resources and publications about body language and nonverbal cues that one would not know where to start if they wanted to improve their body language skills. While the resources on improving body language skills are plentiful it is more important to understand how this skill is applied with specific reference to the Business Analyst practice.

Practice and More Practice

Practice; keep watching your audiences and practice some more, then it will come effortlessly.

Email Management Skills

Next to verbal communications, email (and lately direct messaging via messaging apps) is the main communication tool used by Business Analysts. Not only is it a medium of communication it is also a tool of record that is used to keep track of documents, files, concepts, facts, ideas, and many such artifacts.

Business Analysts spend much of their working days receiving emails, composing emails, sending emails, and making sense of the information in emails. Because email is so central to how Business Analysts work, it is important to consider the ways in which Business Analysts can be more adept, productive, and efficient with the use of email.

Unsurprisingly, there are ways of using email effectively and other ways of using it that are not only ineffective but are guaranteed to invite more work for the Business Analyst.

Here are a couple ways to tell if you are doing email communications all wrong:

- **Emails Invite More Questions**

  When emails invite multiple rejoinders and more questions, it is an indication that the emails lack clarity, are causing confusion, or both. Additionally, when email recipients bring up the email subject in other meetings or anytime they meet the Business Analyst, then the intended message is not getting through.

- **Emails Are Not Read or Opened**

  When email recipients don't bother to read or open emails, then the Business Analyst has an email communication problem. But how do they know their emails are not being read? Being nice to the wonder that is Microsoft Outlook can show them how. It's also obvious emails are going unread if recipients keep asking for email resends.

Emails sent by Business Analysts ought to have these three things: purpose, brevity or conciseness, and clarity if they are going to count as effective emails. Consider this simple email:

"Hello John;

Please confirm if the Sales Team is interested in using a white or gray background for the user interface."

Let's consider why this is an effective email:

- **Purpose**

  The objective of the email is to elicit a response from the recipient, and regardless of the type of response received, the Business Analyst now knows the status of that requirement.

- **Brevity or Conciseness**

  It's short, gets to the point, and it largely requires a yes or no answer. It also gives the receiver the option to respond that they do not know, they are unsure, or they will revert with an answer.

- **Clarity**

  This email is not open to *any* other interpretation; it seeks confirmation from the recipient the direction a requirement will take. This type of email leaves little or zero room for waffling about other unimportant issues.

A good rule of thumb to follow is to keep emails short and the content precise, that way there is no room for the recipients to interpret the email differently from what the Business Analyst intended.

In terms of the addressee (John), it is also very specific about who should respond. Even when the email is addressed to multiple recipients, it is a good idea to address it to a specific recipient who in turn has the responsibility of initiating the response the Business Analyst seeks.

Not all emails are going to be this simple, and there will be occasions when Business Analysts need to stuff a lot of information into a single email. Even in such scenarios, these principles of using email effectively are still applicable.

There are also other ways of ensuring that the use of email is effective and does not become a drag on a Business Analyst's time. Here's how Business Analysts can make email work for them and not the other way around.

How Can Business Analysts Improve This Skill?

Break Long Email Chains

Ever been on an email chain that started last year? Or an email chain so dated that most of those copied have moved to other positions or organizations? Consider yourself lucky if you have not encountered these zombie email chains.

Long running email chains are an indication that the discussion needs to grow legs and find closure by either having a face to face meeting or a phone call that resolves the issue perpetuating the email chain.

Whittle Down Content-Heavy Emails

How about long emails that read like doctoral theses? I understand the need to load an email with all the minutes from the last requirements review meeting, but the Business Analyst ought to ask who is going to read a 30-line email.

They must imagine the 10 minutes a recipient will need to read and understand just that one email. Is it acceptable or reasonable or practical? Not unless you are into sadism.

Granted the minutes need to be sent out, but Business Analysts ought to think through the content of the email and the perceived value it will bring to the recipients. That way they whittle down the content to, for example, only the key takeaways that will ensure that the emails will be read and not redirected to the delete folder.

Another downside of long emails is rework since the recipients don't bother with the details in the emails. They find it convenient to just start new emails or bring those issues up for discussion whenever the opportunity presents itself. Business Analysts should not be in the business of repeatedly explaining emails. It's important to get it right the first time by sending out concise emails that require minimal follow-up or explanations.

Relevant Email Recipients

Much like the discussion on how to run effective meetings, the email recipient list needs to be relevant to the email subject matter. The "To" or "Cc" lists should add recipients who will add value to the email discussion while keeping out recipients with nothing to add to the subject matter.

Keep It Simple

Keep email simple; it shouldn't be complicated. One senior Business Analyst I worked with worked by the motto that emails should be brief and concise to the point where a 5th grader can understand them. Another one swore by the KISS (keep it simple, stupid) principle; remove the fluff and colorful language; just get to the point.

Is Email Right for the Content?

If there is need to disseminate a lot of content and detailed information, that's what email attachments and meetings are for. Emails with brevity can then be used to send out key minutes of what was discussed or future action items.

Visualization

If Business Analysts find that explaining concepts using text generates those long email chains we hate, they can use visualization to get their message across to the audiences. Making use of process maps, charts, diagrams, and screenshots can be used to reach a more visually inclined email audience. This makes explanations far easier than using text with no guarantee they will be understood.

Email Templates

For the tech savvy, some email apps, web apps, and blogs offer professional email templates for the Business Analyst practice. Several enterprise applications that come with email functionality also come embedded with the use of email templates. Business Analysts who make use of these templates are guaranteed to save time while delivering professional emails.

Meetings, Presentation, and Facilitation Skills

The one activity that disproportionately consumes a Business Analyst's time is the attendance and management of meetings and presentations. These are critical activities for Business Analysts for it is how they efficiently broadcast important information to project stakeholders.

These activities incorporate meetings, presentations, joint application design (JAD) sessions, conference calls, web calls, and any other activity that involves dissemination of information to multiple stakeholders at the same time. Some of these activities like requirements discovery/planning/clarification meetings and end user training sessions require direct management by the Business Analyst where he/she delivers presentations or steers the meetings.

Other meetings like technical design meetings, architectural, and technical review meetings will place the Business Analyst in a facilitator role where they convene meetings with technical experts to hash out agreements on direction as well as removing progress blockers.

Meeting Facilitation

In the Business Analyst world, the terms "meeting facilitation or meeting facilitator" are used often, and it refers to Business Analysts creating a safe space where contentious requirements, for example, can be discussed and agreed upon.

Other times the Business Analyst will facilitate a meeting that is convened to resolve conflicts that arise during the project, for example, when development teams stall on component development because it involves significant customizations. The Business Analyst will facilitate such a meeting as a neutral arbiter placed between end users and technical teams with a view to finding a solution that works best for both parties.

Managing Meetings

Inevitably a lot of time goes into managing meeting activities like checking invitee availability, selecting the right invitees, sending invitations, compiling meeting minutes, circulating meeting minutes, and following-up progress on agreed action items.

How Can Business Analysts Improve This Skill?

Given that the management of meetings and presentations takes a significant allotment of a Business Analyst's time, it is important that these activities are managed efficiently and effectively. Here is how that can be done.

Consider the Need for Meetings

Does the Business Analyst need to hold the meeting in the first place? Can the need for a meeting be fulfilled by other means, for example, by email, chat, or one on one meetings? For Business Analysts invited to meetings, they must ask themselves if they need to attend the meeting or consider if there is someone else better placed to attend this meeting.

With the proliferation of collaboration and productivity tools, there are many ways to engage would-be invitees without holding meetings. Business Analysts ought to consider why they need to convene a meeting and more importantly what their expectations are from that meeting. A good rule of thumb is to write out what the meeting should address or resolve as that focuses on the outcomes of the meeting before it is even scheduled.

There is a temptation to conflate holding and attending meetings with actual Business Analyst work; these are very different concepts, and it is important to make this distinction. Depending on the challenges on a project, there is also the pull to hold meetings for every minor insignificant issue. Scheduling too many meetings creates meeting fatigue for end users, stakeholders, and project team members, which is something Business Analysts should avoid. For Business Analysts there is an opportunity cost to attending too many meetings as other aspects of their Business Analyst responsibilities are neglected.

Set an Agenda

As a Business Analyst, I always have reservations about attending a meeting without an agenda, so I make it a point to include an agenda with any meeting I schedule. When managed properly, agendas laser focus meetings on delivering productive outcomes. For good measure a meeting invite should clearly state agenda items so that invitees are aware why they are being invited to the meeting.

For Business Analysts who are the invitees, it is useful to figure out the points of discussion before accepting an invite. If the agenda comes across as lacking in substance, the Business Analyst can request more details before accepting the invite.

Confirm Invitees

Does the meeting have the *right* people in the *right* meeting? Again, this is obvious but still an issue that plagues project meetings. Ideally, Subject Matter Experts or the decision-makers should not only be invited, but they should attend meetings so that they can provide expertise, make decisions, or validate decisions made during the meeting. It's a great idea for Business Analysts to check invitee confirmations especially from end users and stakeholders who are also Subject Matter Experts.

For a Business Analyst who is an invitee, it's a good idea to know who the other invitees are before they confirm their attendance. As an example, if a meeting is convened to discuss technical solutions without the confirmed attendance of a technical team member, that meeting is unlikely to deliver any technical solutions. I cannot think of worse ways to waste precious hours than attend this type of meeting.

Content Prep and Presentation

A key determinant of how productive a meeting or presentation will be is the level of preparation by the Business Analyst. Anticipating and preparing for likely points of contention or disagreement while not foolproof will ensure that the Business Analyst will still have a productive meeting or presentation that moves the project forward. Conversely a lack of preparation and anticipation of problem areas will easily render a meeting unproductive resulting in even more meetings.

Business Analysts need to be well prepared in terms of the subject matter they intend to discuss or present. Projecting confidence in the subject matter naturally comes with being well prepared which also allows the presenter to deliver content concisely and with brevity while staying on message.

As a Business Analyst, there is also a temptation to deliver a lot of content in one meeting or presentation which is understandable given the need to be efficient with time. However, this must be balanced with the need for the invitees to understand the content that is delivered. A nonstop rapid-fire style of delivery does little to help the audience fully grasp the content being presented. As you might have guessed, this leads to more meetings to explain what the invitees did not "understand" the first time out.

Business Analysts also need to compare the content with the time budgeted for the presentation and make the call as to whether the time is enough for that purpose. Failing to do this simplest of tasks usually results in meetings and presentations that go past the allotted time, or another meeting must be set up for a continuation of the same presentation.

Focus on the Purpose of the Meeting

This is different from an itemized agenda and is concerned with whether the meeting has been convened to discuss the problem or the solution. Meetings should be convened to discuss solutions as the invitees should be familiar with the problem or they can be asked to familiarize themselves with the problem *before* they show up for the meeting.

The purpose of the meeting should be to either offer solutions or validate other invitees' solutions. If a meeting is convened to discuss a problem, that part should be kept to a minimum with the larger portion of the meeting dedicated to finding solutions. There is no point in scheduling or attending meetings that dissect problems as it is more important figuring out solutions than discussing the problems themselves. Besides email is a better tool at disseminating information about problems than using meetings to discuss the problems.

This cuts both ways; whether it's the Business Analyst issuing meeting invites or whether they are the ones being invited to a meeting, they ought to be mindful of whether they are going to discuss solutions or problems.

Scheduling

As a Business Analyst who will schedule many meetings during the life of a project, these meeting scheduling pointers are important to keep in mind.

Getting all the invitees in one setting for extended periods of time is easier said than done as end users and stakeholders are busy people with different projects competing for their time. Business Analysts need to be mindful of their time, and if it's possible, contact them beforehand to let them know they are required for meetings. This removes surprises when those invites hit their calendars

There is a need to figure out what meeting cadence works best for meeting invitees. Do they prefer 6-hour meetings or 1-hour daily sessions? It's fair to assume meeting attendees will prefer the latter option as the shorter the meeting, the more focused and invested the invitees will be.

Scheduling too many meetings, meetings crammed in a short space of time, and a reputation for long-winded meetings creates meeting fatigue for end users, stakeholders, and project team members. Predictably they either start being no-shows or outright decline the Business Analysts' invites. There is a need to strike a balance that enables a reasonable number of meetings to be scheduled while also delivering project objectives and removing blockers outside of meetings. While meetings are useful in moving project objectives forward, it does not mean stakeholders will be too thrilled at the thought of their calendars being filled with a Business Analysts' meetings.

Managing the Meeting

What happens once the meeting is underway is just as important as the activities that come before or after meetings. Consider the following elephants in the room where meetings are concerned.

Whether they are the facilitator or presenter, Business Analysts need to watch the clock diligently, and one way is to start the meeting and end it as scheduled. Keep in mind that a meeting that does not cover all the agenda items in the allotted time will require another meeting or an extension of that very meeting. This is how meeting fatigue is created.

Do Business Analysts have the attention of everyone on the call or meeting especially the attention of decision-makers and SMEs? Because if they don't, they will at some point have to repeat the presentation since the audience wasn't paying attention the first time out. It's called rework.

Business Analysts also must nip in the bud any attempt by invitees to sidetrack the meeting by injecting issues that are not on the agenda. Those issues may be relevant, but they are *not* the reason the meeting was convened. Invitees need to be reminded of this etiquette anytime they attempt to hijack a Business Analysts meeting. The Business Analyst can add these "side issues" to the meeting agenda after the main items have been discussed and closed out.

Invitees with a tendency to hog the spotlight with long rambling responses or contributions are some of the reasons why meetings end up being unproductive. Business Analysts can advise the invitee to continue the discussion outside of the meeting also known as taking it offline. Its professional and respectful, and no one's ego gets punctured.

Most importantly Business Analysts need to run meetings with focus and purpose to ensure that the objectives for which the meeting or presentation was convened are achieved.

Highlight Next Steps

A meeting that discussed solutions inevitably has action items or next steps and more importantly the action parties to follow-up those action items within a set timeline. Without timed action items, the meeting might as well have been convened to discuss the weather.

Action parties and expected due dates must be highlighted so that there is follow-up and actual delivery of the action items after the meeting. One underrated upside of following-up and delivering on next steps is that it will likely render a couple of planned future meetings unnecessary or even unproductive.

Additionally, once action parties have completed their commitments, an email is enough to update the audience of the progress made on action items. Business Analysts need to resist the temptation to schedule meetings just to update their audiences on action items progress status.

This is how a Business Analyst can run meetings like a boss. There may be some resistance initially about these methods, but over time Business Analysts will be grateful to themselves for using these pointers to manage their meetings.

These approaches and many more out there in the world of management literature are guaranteed to give Business Analysts back more of their day so that they can juggle other more demanding duties.

Tact and Diplomacy Skills

The ability to communicate with sensitivity and empathy while maintaining relationships is the essence of tact and diplomacy. Human beings can be unpredictable, and situations involving negotiations, persuasion, conflict resolution, or feedback need to be conveyed with an abundance of tact and diplomacy. These can be tense and sensitive situations such that the misinterpretation of a turn of phrase, sentence, or even a nonverbal cue can for instance scuttle a negotiation or a meeting convened to resolve a conflict. While the best Business Analysts understand the importance of tact and diplomatic skills, not many project actors appreciate its application or importance.

Business Analysts who have been in the practice for a while tend to have well-developed tact and diplomatic skills, and here's how those skills manifest in such situations:

- They listen more than they talk, and they let the other party make their points and then fashion a response after that.

- They look out for nonverbal cues that indicate the overall frame of mind of the other party. Are they upbeat, sad, irritated, or upset? This aspect determines the flow of the discussion, and it is vital that Business Analysts align the flow with the disposition of the speaker.

- Based on the flow of a discussion, they carefully chose how to respond in a manner that conveys respect, empathy, and understanding.

It's a common theme on project environments for Business Analysts to "tell it like it is," to be blunt, and to openly say what they are thinking which is great for candidness but does not help with building good relationships. This is precisely where tact and diplomacy need to be deployed.

Business Analysts have to check the manner in which they are "telling it like it is" and whether it is called for in the first place. Telling an end user or stakeholder that the project will make their processes more efficient achieves more goodwill than using derogatory terms to describe their current processes or tools. One statement is positive and looks to the future, while the other is focused on the present, is negative, and is also a thinly veiled denigration of processes that may be dear to stakeholders in spite of their problems.

A key point to note about tact and diplomacy is that it is not the same as flattery or ego stroking. Tact and diplomacy are also not the same as being "soft" or lacking assertiveness. In fact, the skillful use of tact and diplomacy can enable a Business Analyst to leave the negotiation table with what they wanted while at the same time leaving the other party with the impression that they also won.

Here's why tact and diplomacy are important:

- **It Breaks Deadlocks**

  The use of tact and diplomacy can break intractable conflict and negotiations just by a Business Analyst knowing what to say, when to say it, and how to say it. This is done without being brash, judgmental, or in accusatory manner. By hearing out the speakers and then thoughtfully responding Business Analysts, lower temperatures in tense situations and create an environment where respectful and productive discussions can take place.

- **Builds Collaboration and Relationships**

  Given that tact and diplomacy resolve conflicts and close negotiations successfully, they provide the foundation upon which project collaboration thrives. The use of tact prevents the loss of relationships that are vital for collaboration.

How Can Business Analysts Improve This Skill?

Use Communication Skills

The communication skills pointed out in this chapter can be used to defuse tense situations, and they can also be used by Business Analysts to improve their tact and diplomatic craft. Business Analysts can, for example, use active listening, self-awareness, empathy, body language, and the mastery of egos to size up actors in a conflict and know what to say without causing offence, mistrust, or alienation.

Know What, When, and How to Say Something

During negotiations it's of critical importance to do more listening than mindless talking and in order to prevent any "accidents," Business Analysts can write down a set of relevant prepared notes that they will refer to. This eliminates the likelihood that they will present an off-the-cuff position or say something that can be taken out of context and further inflame an already tense situation.

There are other communication skills that Business Analysts will utilize during the process of project delivery, but these are the critical communication skills that Business Analysts will rely on to deliver their assignments. However, this is just one leg out of the three interdependent non-technical skills that this book is concerned with. We now review the second part of that triad.

Interpersonal Skills

The Business Analyst role in its simplest form is that of an intermediary who uses their *mediation* skills to secure agreements from two or more parties that would otherwise not collaborate or work together.

Business Analysts will capture end user requirements, review them, and relay them to software developers so that they can turn those requirements into functional software products.

This process has the potential of requirements getting "lost in translation" and the delivery of a product far removed from what end users ordered. This is not as far-fetched an idea as it seems.

How do Business Analysts inoculate themselves from such monumental mishaps? Part of that answer comes down to the use of interpersonal skills as Business Analysts play the intermediary role in the course of their assignments.

Interpersonal skills refer to the qualities, traits, and behaviors that a Business Analyst uses to interact with end users, stakeholders, and project team members on software development projects. The same instances requiring

© Roni Lubwama 2020
R. Lubwama, *The Inside Track to Excelling As a Business Analyst*,
https://doi.org/10.1007/978-1-4842-5543-8_7

communications skills are also the same instances that require the use of interpersonal skills by Business Analysts, and they are detailed as follows:

- Requirements scoping

- Interactions with technical teams

- Interactions with project stakeholders (end users and project sponsors)

- Situations requiring negotiation, persuasion, and influencing

For our purposes this chapter will focus on a couple of in-demand and frequently used interpersonal skills by Business Analysts. There are other interpersonal skills that have been written about extensively in business and management literature, but for purposes of reviewing what makes excellent Business Analysts, this chapter will focus on six key interpersonal skills.

- **Relationship-Building Skills**

    The Business Analyst as an intermediary has to be capable of cultivating and maintaining relationships between different project actors. Broken relationships are more damaging than helpful to project delivery.

- **Emotional Intelligence**

    This refers to the management of a Business Analyst's emotions as well as those of other project actors. Thrown into this mix is how Business Analysts manage project actors with empathy, understanding, and intelligence.

- **Ego Management**

    Egos are innate to humans, and that's acceptable. Egos, however, cross into unacceptable territory when they run out of control and and start to pose real harm to the process of project delivery.

- **Negotiation and Persuasion**

    An intermediary such as a Business Analyst is not there to play nice; they are there to keep different actors in sync and deliver what is expected of them. This requires a healthy dose of negotiation and persuasive skills.

- **Collaboration**

    Software project delivery relies on the different skillsets and expertise of different actors to bring a project across the finishing line; this objective cannot be accomplished by solo actors. Business Analysts need skills that grow and enhance the collaborative ethic required during the project delivery process.

- **Conflict Management**

  Given the competing interests, visions, objectives, personalities, and egos on a project, conflicts are inevitable. This is when conflict management skills help with defusing these situations.

Relationship-Building Skills

In order for Business Analysts to achieve goals that involve changing mind-sets or when they undertake wide-ranging business process changes, they need to build healthy relationships with end users, stakeholders, and project team members.

The setup and expectations of software development projects make it virtually impossible to deliver without closely working with end users, stakeholders, and project team members.

Because Business Analysts interact with the same faces for a number of months, there is an acceptance that they have to get to know as well as get along with these same project actors. Anything less than this makes the work of project delivery a long experience in pain management for Business Analysts.

The Importance of Building Relationships

The following are the reasons why building relationships is important for successful project delivery.

Amiable Work Relations

It seems fairly obvious, but we all want to work with people who respect us and who we get along with, and Business Analysts are no different.

Business Analysts who conduct themselves professionally and treat team members, end users, and stakeholders respectfully will find that building amiable relations with these actors comes easily. When Business Analysts create amiable relationships, then the hard work of influencing and changing minds becomes much more manageable.

Situations Requiring Negotiation and Persuasion

Negotiations and persuasion are more difficult and imperiled in situations where relationships are weak or strained between Business Analysts and stakeholders, end users, and project team members.

It may seem counterintuitive, but end users and stakeholders are not always in alignment with Business Analysts where requirements and final product delivery are concerned. In instances where Business Analysts need the buy-in and cooperation of intransigent end users and stakeholders, it helps if the Business Analyst has established some sort of working relationship with these actors.

Business Analysts find it very difficult to deliver these objectives if they have strained working relationships with end users and stakeholders that usually stems from inadequate relationship-building efforts.

Conflict Resolution

Investing in building a healthy relationship will be fully paid back when conflict resolution time comes around. Because a Business Analyst has conducted themselves professionally and depicted positive social behaviors, they can step into conflict situations and defuse them.

They can resolve conflicts because they have healthy working relationships with the conflicting parties, the absence of which makes it a much harder task to achieve.

How Can Business Analysts Build and Maintain Relationships?

Active Listening

A Business Analyst with a known penchant for not listening or ignoring those speaking to him/her will encounter serious difficulties with building relationships.

Championing Stakeholder Needs

This does not mean that all end user requirements will be considered; for instance, it just means that a Business Analyst is genuinely interested in their pain points. Getting pain points and eliciting requirements from end users and stakeholders calls for genuinely and actively listening to them.

When stakeholders and end users are of the opinion that the Business Analyst is working on resolving their problems, then that Business Analyst will have an easy time building relationships with them.

Usually this opinion does not come out of the blue; end users and stakeholders will have seen firsthand the efforts undertaken by the Business Analysts to bring a resolution to their pain points.

Helping end users and stakeholders is not to be conflated with agreeing to their every whim and demand. Business Analysts can respectfully and professionally shelve some requests which garners the admiration and trust of end users and stakeholders that are essential to relationship building.

Professionalism

Treating stakeholders, end users, and project team members with respect and professionalism during moments of disagreements or during the discussion of contentious issues helps build or maintain relationships in project settings. It is the knowledge when to tactfully disagree with stakeholders, end users, and project team members in a way that does not leave them feeling belittled or disrespected.

A common scenario is end users who keep churning out requirements (scope creep). A good response is not to shut them down by saying "Forget it; we are not adding any more requirements" but by letting them know they have been heard and these requirements will be reviewed by the wider team at the appropriate time.

This response engenders respect for the Business Analyst and maintains a healthy rapport with end users instead of leaving them dissatisfied and disrespected at the same time.

Willingness to Learn

Showing vulnerability and a willingness to learn the business and processes of end users and stakeholders softens the barriers to relationship building. Conversely, a Business Analyst who comes off as a "knows it all" to end users and stakeholders is going to have a hard time building relationships with them.

Business Analysts who exhibit "know-it-all attitudes" run the risk of being seen as disrespectful and unwilling to learn so that they can help end users and stakeholders banish their problems.

It's also probably the worst way a Business Analyst could start off any relationship with end users or stakeholders on projects.

Communication

Keeping everyone in the information loop whether it is good or bad news that they need to know is a good way to build and maintain relationships. As a Business Analyst, eliminating surprises especially preventable ones is guaranteed to build stronger relationships.

It confers an aura of openness and transparency upon a Business Analyst which aids relationship building efforts.

Positive Attitudes

Staying positive even in dark times is a good cultivator of relationships. A negative person with a "the sky is falling" attitude will not win over many stakeholders, end users, and project team members.

It is more useful to fashion practical solutions that help stabilize the project than dabbling in fear mongering and general negativity.

The Business Analyst is there to generate solutions not compound problems, and most end users, stakeholders, and project team members are easier to build relationships with by displaying a positive disposition.

Deliver on Commitments

Business Analysts who deliver on what they commit to will build stronger relationships with stakeholders, end users, and project team members.

The flip side is Business Analysts who fall behind on their commitments or don't keep their promises engender mistrust, a lack of credibility, and eventually broken relationships.

Emotional Intelligence

How does a Business Analyst respond when a stakeholder or end user says something so untrue or so grossly taken out of context it ends up throwing serious shade at him/her and their requirements?

Chances are they will be outraged, seething, and in the mood to strangle the speaker. How do they respond to this situation? Do they rescue their shredded reputation by immediately putting up a spirited defense of themselves? Assuming that is the chosen path, is there a guarantee that they will decouple their emotions from that defense and maintain the professional demeanor and intelligent response that the moment requires?

That is unlikely.

More likely their defense and emotions will be fused, and what their audience is likely to see is an angry emotive response. Never mind that what appears as an emotive response actually addresses some legitimate points.

There is a second way.

The Business Analyst can wait until their anger has dissipated then offer a response or rebuttal of the factually inaccurate information presented by the stakeholder. For some people, that cooling-down period can be a few minutes, while others may need a few hours to compose themselves and come up with a response.

Guess which approach appears more professional, restrained, calm, and confers admiration upon the Business Analyst in this situation?

The second way is the clear winner here, and it is the essence of emotional intelligence which is defined as the ability to manage one's emotions as well as handling other people's emotions and situations empathetically.

Emotional intelligence has upsides like the creation of collaborative spaces that contribute to successful project delivery. On the flip side, actors exhibiting negative emotional intelligence foster a non-collaborative project atmosphere that sooner rather than later jams the wheels of successful project delivery.

Business Analysts who consistently deliver successful projects tend to have high emotional intelligence skills. At the end of the spectrum low emotional intelligence Business Analysts struggle with project delivery especially when it comes to managing and relating with other actors on project teams.

This is how both high and low emotional intelligence is manifested.

Signs of High Emotional Intelligence and Its Impacts

Possessing an abundance of emotional intelligence skills is more than a cherry on the pie for Business Analysts for they manage people better especially during crisis situations. These are the signs of a Business Analyst rich in emotional intelligence.

Self-Awareness and Self-Control

High emotional intelligence Business Analysts are aware of their emotions and know when to restrain themselves. In the above scenario, the Business Analyst would hold eye contact with the stakeholder and let them speak to the end.

They realize that anger or defensiveness (in the moment) will detract from the speaker's content. That content however ill-conceived still needs to be heard.

Empathy

Business Analysts rich in empathy mentally engage in role-play which is putting themselves in the "shoes" of an actor like a stakeholder. When a stakeholder expresses frustration with, for instance, the requirements scoping process, the Business Analyst actively listens not because the stakeholder is correct but because role-playing enables the Business Analyst to understand the stakeholder's frustrations.

Perspective and Insight

Allied to empathy is the ability to use deeper perspectives and insights that shine a different light on intractable problems.

That developer who won't undertake a requirement because it requires learning a new programming language is not afraid of the new language; they are just twitchy about learning and delivering the requirement at the same time. It turns out to be more of a time management issue than an issue about the developer's abilities. This is the kind of perspective that high emotional intelligence enables.

Curious and Open Minded

Closely tied to the ability to embrace change is the ability to be curious and stay open minded about problems and solutions alike.

Project team members may offer impractical solutions, but high emotional intelligence Business Analysts are curious to hear how the solution will work as opposed to shutting down the discussion saying; "I have heard that before, and it does not work."

In this instance the proposed solution may not be applicable, but it could be applicable for another problem elsewhere or at another time.

Social Skills

Emotionally intelligent Business Analysts prize social skills because they are the glue that builds relationships and enables them to understand the different dispositions of project team members, end users, and stakeholders.

Positive with a Sunny Disposition

The challenges on projects especially those with tight deadlines, grumpy actors, and fluid requirements to mention a few can dampen the moods of even the most positive project team member.

However, Business Analysts cannot fall prey to this "sky is falling" syndrome which is interpreted as the project will fail regardless of what the project team does.

In a way Business Analysts are the troop leaders, and they cannot manifest a defeatist mentality to other project actors or else those project actors start to exhibit the same defeatist mentalities in their project assignments.

Granted, there will be multiple challenges on a project, but the best Business Analysts know that this is just "another day at the office" and that they will succeed as long as they are focused on resolving the challenges.

The high emotional intelligence Business Analyst also understands that change is a constant and they embrace the changes or enable the changes to be successfully implemented. They prepare for the changes the best they can, keep adjusting, and stay positive despite the challenges.

They keep their eyes on the prize regardless of the storms around them.

Confident and Self-Assured

In addition to a positive disposition, the best Business Analysts are also confident and self-assured about themselves.

They know they will occasionally make mistakes, but they don't let those mishaps define them. To them it's just another bad day as long as they do better the following day.

In league with self-assuredness is not holding on to grudges. This is especially relevant in those instances where they have to work with feisty and abrasive stakeholders or end users. Sometimes encounters with these stakeholders go very badly, and Business Analyst may want to "red flag" such actors which eventually harms the relationships.

Ace Business Analysts focus on working with these actors, building functional relationships with them, and learning to treat their prickly personalities as side shows.

Signs of Low Emotional Intelligence and Its Impacts

As humans we don't always have the right sets of emotional intelligence skills, and the paucity of these skills can make for a bumpy project delivery process. These are the instances of low emotional intelligence in Business Analysts and how they impact the project delivery process.

Poor or Inadequate Emotional Control

We all know folks who lose control, and Business Analysts are no different as sometimes stakeholders and end users can be so irritating that a Business Analyst who loses their cool can be empathized with.

Unfortunately, such irritating moments are not the place nor timing for a Business Analyst to lose control.

Lack of Self-Awareness, Empathy, and Tone Deafness

A lack of self-awareness by a Business Analyst certainly signals low emotional intelligence.

A Business Analyst who has difficulty accepting negative feedback, does not gauge nonverbal cues, and is mainly interested in their opinions is suffering from a serious lack of self-awareness.

Then there are Business Analysts who value efficiency over empathy and will not, for example, hesitate to shut down an end user discussion because the Business Analyst believes the discussion is a waste of time.

This attitude only engenders mistrust, anger, and frustration with the Business Analyst and which in due course damages the collaborative ethic of a project as well as the relationships critical to project success. It's true that stakeholder discussions may sometimes be repetitive and a waste of time, but there are emotionally intelligent ways of managing this discussion other than just shutting it down in the name of efficiency and time management.

Poor Relationship Management Skills

Like in other aspects of our lives, relationships are cultivated and maintained when we manage them by being emotionally intelligent. A lack of empathy or respect toward stakeholders and project team members for instance is not going to help a Business Analyst build the type of relationships that are essential for collaboration and successful project delivery.

Importance of Emotional Intelligence

Having the right set of emotional intelligence skills is important on software development projects for it helps with effectively managing project actors and crisis situations better which leads to better project delivery outcomes. This is why Business Analysts need emotional intelligence skills.

Builds Resilience

Emotional intelligence helps Business Analysts build resilience that can mitigate and prevent Business Analysts from going into meltdown modes. Resilient Business Analysts know that their requirements will be scrutinized to the point of the scrutiny taking on the appearance of the personal. To them this is just "another day at the office" and not worth having a meltdown over.

Needless to say, episodes that demonstrate a lack of emotional control also demonstrate an unprofessional Business Analyst.

Enhances Nuanced Perspectives

Emotional intelligence equips Business Analysts with nuanced perspectives that are essential in gaining "behind the scenes" insights into challenges that may arise during project delivery.

End users who are not using a newly deployed application are not just rebellious; they are probably skeptical that it will make their work simpler, or maybe they need more training to give them the confidence required for adoption.

Without a nuanced perspective borne of emotional intelligence that considers the end user's side of the story, the Business Analyst is likely to conclude that the end users are merely rebellious holdouts.

Challenges are seen as opportunities to address underlying problems by, for example, asking if the issue is one of mind-sets, resources, stakeholder support, project scope, or even external factors.

There is usually more than meets the eye with these challenges, and it requires emotional intelligence to understand what's going on.

Enhances Learning Opportunities from Problems

Emotionally intelligent Business Analysts use challenges as learning opportunities, and they know if they look deeper, they are going to learn why their project has to contend with a stream of never-ending challenges.

Business Analysts focusing on the drama arising from these situations will miss these learning opportunities.

Less Focus on Personal Frustrations

Emotionally intelligent Business Analysts resist the temptation to focus on their feelings of frustration and negativity when the list of obstacles arraigned against a project seem to be never-ending.

Focusing on the negativity produced by constant firefighting is human, but sadly it takes the focus away from the problems and more importantly the required solutions.

Improves Interpretation of Situations and Actions

Business Analysts are no different from us when they handle particularly irritating end users, and some Business Analysts' default positions may be to mentally and physically shut down such infuriating end users.

While it may be convenient in the moment, shutting down the discussion does not remove the reason why they are irritating in the first place.

High–emotional intelligence Business Analysts "get" that these end users are irritating for a *reason*. They may a have pain point so bad that being irritating is perhaps the only way of getting a quick resolution.

A healthy dose of emotional intelligence equips Business Analysts to see these situations for what they are: cries for help.

Builds Better Relationships

Another one that does not need to be stated but which will be stated, nonetheless.

Emotional intelligence builds self-awareness which equips Business Analysts with the knowledge they need to cultivate relationships with different project actors.

With this knowledge Business Analysts know which behaviors they need to tamp down or which ones they need to express more as they seek the attention or cooperation of end users, stakeholders, and project team members.

Being emotionally intelligent gives Business Analysts the skills they need to gauge project situations and how to navigate them. Stakeholders being difficult? Maybe it's best to socialize with them on issues other than just project work.

Perhaps end users and stakeholders share the same hobbies or the same interests as the Business Analyst. These shared experiences create the foundation for building relationships that engender collaboration during project delivery.

Conflict Management and Collaboration Enhancement

This seems obvious but still needs to be stated; low emotional intelligence Business Analysts are likely to engender even more conflicts on project teams by their lack of self-awareness and general lack of empathy.

It's only natural that a Business Analyst lacking in self-awareness of their destructive personality will find resistance instead of collaboration.

Business Analysts who are emotionally intelligent also take the time to study who they are working with as well as gain social insights into different project actors. They understand what makes some team members produce their best work and what does not and adjust accordingly. This cannot be done without generous doses of self-awareness and empathy.

Enhances Communication and Openness

High emotional intelligence Business Analysts are self-assured of their abilities and understand that what is important is not necessarily their feelings but achieving the wider project objectives.

To that end they prize open communications even when those communications sometimes don't bring good news. Emotionally intelligent Business Analysts take the perspective that while they may look "bad" in the moment, this is what needs to be done. This attitude builds credibility and trust with different actors on projects.

Helps with Influencing and Persuasion

Ever tried influencing a person who just saw you have an angry meltdown or someone you humiliated in the past but because you were deficient in self-awareness did not even realize what you had done?

Those negotiations will be dead in the water.

Low emotional intelligence Business Analysts have a hard time trying to influence, negotiate with, or persuade other project actors especially if their personalities create avoidable conflicts or damage relationships.

When people are belittled, humiliated, or disrespected, they tend to remember those moments when Business Analysts need their assistance the most.

Helps with Decision-Making

High emotional intelligence Business Analysts remove their emotions when making critical decisions. A Business Analyst who is convinced a stakeholder does not like him or her personally since that stakeholder was asking "embarrassing or difficult" questions is not in the right state of mind to make impartial decisions related to that stakeholder.

Is there a guarantee that this Business Analyst will keep their emotions or "hurt" feelings out of those types of decisions? Of course not.

High emotional intelligence Business Analysts understand that these kinds of decisions are best made by removing emotions from the decision-making process. Bringing that baggage into a decision-making process is unlikely to lead to good decisions.

Recognition of Power Politics

Business Analysts need to be well-equipped with emotional intelligence so that they can discern the "hidden" meanings of project actor actions.

There will be instances when the actions of project actors are meant to "play to the gallery," engage in power struggles, seek to impress other actors, show who is boss, play "smarty pants," or generally just being a jerk.

Emotional intelligence is what clues Business Analysts onto these distractions and more importantly gives them the ammunition they need to neutralize them.

The flip side is that a Business Analyst lacking the nuances of emotional intelligence can easily fall for these sideshows and exacerbate their impacts instead of mitigating them.

How Business Analysts Can Improve Their Emotional Intelligence Skills

Emotional intelligence has lately garnered a lot of attention in the business press, and there are countless reference sources that can help Business Analysts improve their emotional intelligence abilities. Nonetheless here are a few tried and tested methods that can just as ably improve emotional intelligence for Business Analysts.

Practicing Role-Play

This is not an easy one, but taking a step back and using role-play or stepping into the "shoes" of end users, stakeholders, and project team members improves the ability to view a situation as someone else. This ability is central to building empathetic abilities, and Business Analysts will be well-served by role-playing as a way of improving emotional intelligence.

Know Thyself

As humans we come equipped with both good and bad personalities, and some of these personality traits are injurious to project collaboration as well as being offensive to end users, stakeholders, and project team members.

Can we avoid being frustrated, angry, or being irritable? Of course not.

The key is being cognizant of the triggers of these behaviors and figuring out remedial measures that temper our darker impulses especially during critical interactions with end users, stakeholders, and project team members.

A Business Analyst feeling flustered and irritated during a meeting with a stakeholder can stay calm and let the stakeholder do the talking as their feelings of irritability subside. By doing this they can respond at precisely the time they are calm while making intelligent and reasoned rejoinders as opposed to responding while carrying the baggage of irritability.

Accountability

Sometimes project situations are so dire that Business Analysts cannot avoid lapsing into low emotional intelligence territory. When that happens the best course of action is for Business Analysts to own it, be accountable for what happened, and endeavor not to have repeat behaviors in the future.

Avoiding accountability and not learning from these experiences virtually guarantees that these behaviors will recur; after all the Business Analyst did not consider what happened worth atoning for.

Active Listening

Business Analysts in the market for improved emotional intelligence abilities ought to start with the low technology and frequently disregarded skill of active listening.

All it takes is to actively listen and leverage role-play to understand the thinking processes of end users, stakeholders, and project team members.

Leverage Social Skills and Self-Awareness

This entails using social skills to understand end users, stakeholders, and project team members, what they like and dislike, or what brings out their best and what doesn't. It's all about using self-awareness and social skills to improve emotional intelligence with regard to the actors a Business Analyst frequently interacts with on a project.

Ego Management

Managing egos is a key issue for Business Analysts, stakeholders, end users, and project team members as it can stifle project progress if it isn't nipped in the bud early.

Ego plays are not to be conflated with the intellectual abilities of any of these actors as these are two different concepts.

Egoism on project settings is essentially putting individual self-centered needs before project objectives, and this is how out of control egos are manifested on projects.

How Are Egos Manifested on Projects?

Denial of Reality

This is when a Business Analyst has difficulty accepting that they are using flawed logic or assumptions during requirements scoping, for instance. They insist on using the same logic even when they have been shown the flaws in this logic.

Hogging the Limelight

Those situations when Business Analysts do all the talking and the audience especially stakeholders or end users are not given the opportunity to meaningfully contribute to discussions.

It is also manifested when Business Analysts want to have a say on every topic of discussion even when they have nothing of substance to contribute to the discussion.

This situation is by no means specific to Business Analysts, and stakeholders are just as guilty of hogging the limelight. For stakeholders it is made worse when they carry the attitude that they are the only ones who can authoritatively discuss requirements or insisting on having all their requirements reviewed whether they are important or not.

Impervious to Change

This is when Business Analysts show themselves incapable or unwilling to learn concepts that will make them change their views or be accepting of new viewpoints. They are inflexible in their viewpoints even when they are presented with new ideas or alternative perspectives.

Having the "Last Word" Syndrome

Business Analysts who want to be right all the time and have the urge to always have the last word on a discussion. This may be further manifested by Business Analysts who are patronizing toward end users and stakeholders working on the notion that the Business Analyst understands end user requirements better than stakeholders.

Lack of Self Awareness

This is when Business Analysts lack the self-awareness that recognizes how their behavior or conduct is inconveniencing or downright discomforting to others in their midst.

Consider a situation where a Business Analyst follows a line of argument during a meeting that everyone can see is flawed. This is a distraction from the purpose of the meeting, and it prevents meaningful discussions from taking place as a result of the Business Analyst's lack of self-awareness. This is not unique to Business Analysts as stakeholders are just as guilty of this type of egoism.

Personalization of Issues

This is when Business Analysts or stakeholders consider a rebuttal of their ideas or requirements as a personal attack on them.

Self-Centered Stakeholders

This is usually the case when stakeholders treat software products, processes, or applications as their turf and are not fully cooperative or receptive when changes are proposed.

Obviously, this is harmful to project collaboration efforts not to mention that it puts the project at risk of not meeting its objectives.

Effects of Egoism on Projects

Managing egos on a project may be thought of as an insignificant issue, but too many out of control egos on a project can slow down project delivery and here's how.

Impedes Project Progress

Let's review a scenario where a Business Analyst is informed that they missed a couple of requirements and that they need to add these requirements to the scope. Alternatively, consider a stakeholder who refuses to sign off requirements that will change their processes because they still believe in the adequacy of the current processes and don't appreciate the need to change them.

These sound like straightforward scenarios, but in both the egos of both actors have taken center stage, and project progress is stalled because the actors either believe they will "look bad" or they don't want to give the impression that their processes are inefficient.

Suffocates Communication

Because project actors want to dominate meetings and presentations, the intention of communicating important content is frustrated. This is because the egoists do most of the talking with limited active listening on their part meaning that the audience is given minimal or zero opportunities to meaningfully contribute to the dialogue. These actions inevitably result in a cycle of never-ending meetings seeking this information.

Damages Collaboration

Egoists hell-bent on defending their "turf" or whatever they consider a cause worth defending end up suffocating the spirit of project collaboration, which is essential for project delivery. Who wants to work on requirements that won't be signed off by an aggrieved stakeholder? Business Analysts certainly don't relish working with such stakeholders.

Not to mention that these ego turf wars are likely to exacerbate conflicts, create mistrust, and generally poison the spirit of collaboration on projects.

How Can Business Analysts Get a Handle on Egos?

This is how a Business Analyst can control their own ego as well as manage the egos of project stakeholders, end users, and other project team members

For Business Analysts

Openness to New Ideas, Concepts, and Perspectives

Ace Business Analysts understand that they don't always have the best ideas and usually don't suffer from "smartest person in the room" syndrome. They recognize that being receptive to other ideas, concepts, and perspectives places them in a better position to understand end user pain points.

Don't Treat Criticism As Personal

Unless the rebuttal of a Business Analyst's ideas is directed at them personally or their personal shortcomings, there is no reason a rebuttal or critique of their ideas should be treated as an affront to their person.

While Business Analysts may have difficulty with scrutiny of requirements that dings their egos, this process is necessary to improve requirements and close information gaps.

Self-Awareness

Growing in self-awareness is harder than it sounds but not impossible to achieve. Self-awareness allows Business Analysts to be cognizant of the impact of their actions on their audiences.

Self-awareness can be improved by getting honest feedback from project team members, for example, on how Business Analysts conduct meetings or presentations.

Using Communication Skills

Business Analysts can get a handle on their personal egos by looking out for body language signals during interactions with audiences.

Is the audience bored in meetings? Possibly so and that could be because the Business Analyst is the only one doing the talking. They could be bored because the meeting has turned into a sermon instead of a discussion. Are the audiences tuning out the Business Analyst? Maybe. This could be arising from a Business Analyst high on "smartest person in the room" syndrome.

For Stakeholders, End Users, and Project Team Members

Provide Genuine Feedback

Business Analysts ought to give feedback through Project Managers or Project Sponsors about stakeholders, end users, and project team members with out of control egos. The feedback should be professional and focused on how the egos are impeding the project or stifling collaboration.

Role-Play

As a Business Analyst, dealing with ocean-sized egos can feel insurmountable, but a bit of role-play—putting yourself in the egoist's "shoes"—can provide insights on why the egoists are exhibiting these behaviors. These insights can then provide avenues of resolving the egoist's pain points.

Imagine a stakeholder in the grip of "smartest person in the room" syndrome; they have all the answers, and they feel they are the only ones who can discuss a given subject authoritatively. A Business Analyst could ask themselves what the point of all this showboating is. Maybe the stakeholder is seeking public recognition or adulation of their knowledge, or its probable they want to catch the attention of other senior stakeholders.

The Business Analyst can channel this ego to efforts that actually help the project (if it's within their authority). The egomaniac can, for example, be given an assignment to detail application entity relationship diagrams and thereafter deliver a presentation about their assignment.

This is a win-win situation; the egoist gets to flaunt their ego (plus deep expertise), and the project team members get to benefit from the delivery of new information.

Flag As a Risk

If decisions are being stifled due to egoistical tuff wars, then this needs to be flagged as a project risk. Flagging it as a risk gives the issue visibility and creates opportunities for the turf wars to be resolved in concert with other team members and stakeholders.

Escalation

If end users and stakeholders are the ones exhibiting destructive egoistical behaviors and engaging in territorialism, a Business Analyst has few tools for resolution short of diplomatically escalating the issue to project leadership or organizational management.

Emphasize Project Team Collaboration

Emphasizing the value of collaborative efforts on a project team may not eliminate egoistical behaviors, but it sends the message that "we are in this together."

It's a given that project actors will have egos, some more destructive than others, but it's important to send out the message that the team will deliver results due to collaboration not in spite of it.

It's OK to have larger than life egos, but they have to check their egos at the door every morning for the good of the project.

Communication Skills and Tools

Active listening, body language cues, and meeting management skills can be used by Business Analysts to rein in destructive egos. By, for instance, setting ground rules for meetings, egos can be controlled, and everyone gets the opportunity to be heard.

When Business Analysts facilitate meetings, they can use nonverbal cues to sense when an audience is out of sync with an egotistical presenter and step in to reset the meeting in real time.

Negotiation and Persuasion

Business Analysts encounter many challenges during the life span of a project that are resolved largely by the use of negotiations and persuasive abilities. These abilities, however, work in tandem with technical skills as well as communication and problem-solving skills to deliver the outcomes that Business Analysts seek.

For the purposes of this book, the skills and powers of negotiation, persuasion, and influencing will be considered as one skill as they achieve the same result: changing the minds and actions of end users, stakeholders, and project team members.

Take a case where end users request a software product but for reasons like budget, time, resourcing, or other unplanned events, a "lite" version of the product is what will be delivered. The delivered product works, but it's not exactly what the end users requested.

Another variation of this scenario is when Business Analysts scope requirements and ask the technical team to review the requirements. Upon review it turns out that while the product will be delivered eventually, it will be a very complex delivery and will likely be delivered outside the original timelines.

The Business Analyst therefore has to persuade both sets of parties to accept outcomes they had not planned for or envisaged. In the first scenario, the Business Analyst will have to negotiate with end users and stakeholders to accept the delivery of a software product that is different from the one envisioned by the requirements scoping process. In the second scenario, the negotiations undertaken by the Business Analyst will likely center around extending the project timeline so as to deliver the complex product. Obviously, this involves the sticky point of cost implications, and the negotiations have to be done in concert with project leadership.

How Can Business Analysts Master the Negotiation Game?

Prioritizing End User Needs and Requirements

By putting end user needs front and center of the negotiation pitch, Business Analysts put themselves in a better position to have successful negotiations. The Business Analyst can show end users how a product different from what was requested in the requirements will fulfill their requirements and the work-arounds that can be used to meet unfulfilled requirements. This attitude indicates to end users that the Business Analyst literally has their back and they are generally more inclined to go along with the proposals on the table.

Conversely if end users get the impression that the Business Analyst has not given deep thought to how this alternative product will deliver their requirements, those negotiations are going to be difficult if not a downright failure.

End users and stakeholders are usually fearful (and with good reason) of the risks inherent in accepting a product that is different from what they requested. Will their processes become even more broken? Are they getting the efficiencies they need to stay competitive? These are some of the questions that indicate the fears end users and stakeholders have toward what the Business Analyst is selling. It is important for Business Analysts to think through these risks and develop mitigation work-arounds if they are going to have successful negotiations.

Using Trust and Credibility

Would you be persuaded by someone you do not trust? How about conducting negotiations with someone who is not exactly credible based on past interactions with them? Negotiations that Business Analysts have to engage in with end users and stakeholders are no different. Business Analysts who have shown themselves unable to meet their commitments in the past with end users are going to have a hard time during negotiations with them. The negotiations are difficult for the simple reason that end users and stakeholders don't know if they can trust the Business Analyst given what they already know about him or her.

Moral of the story: keeping commitments and delivering end user needs are what build trust and credibility, and that currency is very vital during negotiations.

Figuring Out Influential Actors

It's not difficult to figure out who wields the most influence or clout on a team of end users or stakeholders. While it is important to conduct negotiations with teams of end users or stakeholders, it is vital to figure out the person on those teams with the most influence—that person whose "yes" or "no" has the most clout. If the Business Analyst can identify this person of influence and genuinely seek to build a rapport with them, they have an opportunity to turn difficult negotiations into manageable ones. Usually this person of influence can convince the holdouts on the team to accept the Business Analysts' negotiation points. Think of it as a domino effect: persuade the key players, and they will persuade the other members of their teams.

Preparation for Negotiations

I have observed Business Analysts who prepare for negotiations as if they were preparing battle plans. They anticipate points of contention, possible flash points, feisty or spiky stakeholders, flawed arguments, historical precedents, and many other such morsels of information. It's not that Business Analysts love the minutiae of who knifed the negotiations last time around; they just want to cover as many of their bases as they can and not leave themselves exposed. This homework is helpful as not only can it get difficult negotiations out of jail but it can also soften stakeholders who can see that the Business Analyst has "thought this thing through." When a Business Analyst is well-prepared, even stakeholders and end users who are perpetual naysayers find it difficult to turn down well-crafted arguments and counterarguments—unless there are other issues at play behind the scenes.

Product and Solution Confidence

Closely following on preparation is confidence in what the Business Analyst is selling and their knowledge about the product. A car salesman who cannot tell you the mileage per gallon of a car they are selling is either a poor salesman or is uninterested in selling the car or both. It's the same analogy with a Business Analyst who negotiates with end users or stakeholders who will naturally want to know about the products on the negotiation table. Take, for example, a Business Analyst who tells end users they cannot get their application with five functions, but they will get it with two. As might be expected, end users want to know what the latter option will do for them and more importantly which requirements it will fulfill or not fulfill. This is when it's not just general product knowledge that is important but knowledge of the proposed solution and the conviction that it is well-suited to the requirements of the moment that is even more important. End users won't sign off these negotiations if they detect hesitation or a lack of confidence in the product or solution being sold by the Business Analyst.

Communication Best Practices

Difficult and "not going anywhere" negotiations can be turned into success stories by the style of communication. Are stakeholders having a hard time internalizing a 50-page document? How about visualizing parts of that information by using process maps, charts, and diagrams? Is the language too technical? Then the communication needs to be tailored to the audience. Is the Business Analyst doing all the talking and very little listening leading to the audience tuning out the Business Analyst? It's time to take a back seat and do some active listening. A negotiation pitch ought to follow communication best practices if the Business Analyst is going to get their message through. Keep it simple, stupid (KISS) works wonders in negotiations: keep things simple, no fluff, jargon, or gimmickry.

Enlist the Experts and Pros

It can be tempting to go solo when negotiating with stakeholders given that there is always the payoff of the glory that comes with individually putting difficult negotiations to bed. That said, this is a dangerous strategy that can backfire spectacularly.

Relying on project team members with deeper expertise is a more prudent way to get intransigent end users and stakeholders to accept what the Business Analyst is selling. End users and stakeholders asking painful and unexpected questions can be taken care of by the intellectual heavyweights that have accompanied the Business Analyst to the negotiation table. That's precisely why the Business Analyst brought them—to bat away those painful questions. The other point is that stakeholders seeing the intellectual muscle arraigned before them get the impression that the Business Analyst takes their business seriously and wants to see them succeed. The experts on a project team can also be called on to validate and check the negotiation proposal before the Business Analysts presents it before stakeholders.

This scenario also works for negotiation scenarios where the project timeline has to be extended which means the stakeholders are likely to fork over more money for the project. In those instances, it's advisable to bring in the project managers or project sponsors to do the heavy lifting as they have a bigger picture view of project budgets and expenditures, while Business Analyst handle the tactical issues of the negotiations.

The wider point here is for the Business Analyst to know where the negotiation and persuasion efforts are jammed and which expertise to bring in to break the deadlock.

Avoid the Hard Sell

The other temptress that Business Analysts fall for is to try and go for the hard sell; they go into a negotiation room with the intention of leaving the room with pen put to paper—they intend to close the negotiation come hell or high water.

Business Analysts in this situation can be empathized with when schedules are tight and milestones need to be signed off as completed. In such situations, going for the hard sell maybe the only realistic way to get compliance. However, this is usually counterproductive as stakeholders tend to view the hard sell as a sign of Business Analyst or project desperation. They also interpret the effort to get the sign off via the hard sell as overriding their concerns.

If anything, the hard sell is likely to make difficult negotiations even more difficult. In those catch-22 situations, its best for Business Analysts to just lay out the facts, arguments, case studies, best practices, and best of both worlds scenarios and give stakeholders time to make the right call.

If All Else Fails

Sometimes none of these strategies will work however hard or astutely a Business Analyst deploys them, and the only option left is to wheel out the Gatling guns. At this point, the project managers or project champions need to step in and break the deadlock maybe by making a few concessions that are within their remit. However, this is a last resort measure, and it's best deployed when the Business Analyst has practically tried everything under the sun as well as documented why those actions did not work.

Collaboration

Software product development is centered on self-organizing and matrixed teams that largely rely on collaboration to deliver software products.

If you think this is hyperbole, try envisioning a situation where a Business Analyst delivers a requirement from start to finish without the intervention of developers or test engineers. You don't have to go far into this mental exercise to see that its impractical simply because it goes against the rationale of using project teams for product development. That rationale is to leverage the different functional roles, skillsets, expertise, and personalities on a project within a collaborative setting to efficiently deliver functional software products to end users.

The teams are matrixed because different roles bring a diversity of skillsets and abilities to a project team. As an example, in addition to the usual crew of developers, architects, and Business Analysts, a project team is reliant on Subject Matter Experts sourced from different departments of the organization to provide expertise toward the project.

Once they are thrown together on a project, the team members have to develop a collaborative ethos that brings out the best in them. Think of it as a pooling of talents, skills, and expertise to serve the wider objective of project deliverables.

Without this collaborative ethos, a project team is made up of individuals who individually cannot deliver project objectives. This collaborative ethic binds the team together, and, in that way, they are an insurmountable force that not only delivers project objectives but also overcomes the usual obstacles and challenges along the way.

It may be tempting to think of building a team collaboration ethic as the responsibility of the Project Matter, but that is a superficial assessment, and Business Analysts are just as responsible for fostering collaboration as Project Managers.

Why Is Collaboration Important for Project Teams?

Problem-Solving Capabilities

Teams in collaborative settings are better suited to confront the myriad challenges that project teams encounter in the software development process. The different skillsets and functional roles can be leveraged to creatively solve problems and sustain project momentum. However, for this to happen, that team has to have already attained a collaborative and cohesive structure. It is difficult to consistently solve problems and remove blockers when team members do not collaborate or where there is zero sense of shared purpose.

Product Delivery

Guess who coined this saying, "Talent wins games but teamwork and intelligence win championships"?[1] I will save you the bother; the answer is in the footnote. This sage knows a thing or two about team collaboration and its impact on delivering big prizes. Building a collaborative and cohesive project team is a better vehicle for software product delivery than instructing one person to see the process through from start to finish. Building a collaboration ethic then focuses the team on the bigger picture which is delivering a functional product to end users.

How Can Business Analysts Improve Collaboration on Project Teams?

The spirit of team collaboration and cohesion is compromised where the following behaviors are exhibited by Business Analysts on project teams. The end result is that some team members and stakeholders view themselves as "outside" the project team and don't see the value of aligning themselves to the mission of the project.

---

[1] www.forbes.com/sites/grantfreeland/2018/06/01/talent-wins-games-teamwork-wins-championships/#3731db44c8f1

Team Player Leading from the Front

Business Analysts come into this role fully aware that a lot of their work is going to be delivered through teamwork and collaborative efforts. The Business Analyst has to lead from the front by demonstrating that they are team players and that they work collaboratively. If they ask team members to work as a team but they are personally not invested in working with other team members, then the collaborative ethic on that project is weakened. It reminds me of a Business Analyst I worked with once who was quick to bask in the limelight when the project was doing alright but equally quick to blame individual team members anytime things were going sideways. Your guess is as good as mine as to what happened to the collaboration ethic on that team.

Information Sharing

Selective sharing of information harms the collaborative ethic of software project delivery. Business Analysts who provide information to perceived "buddies" while excluding other project team members from this information loop do a major disservice to collaboration on project teams. If there is information concerning project progress, then Business Analysts ought to share it with the project team, and if they must share information selectively, then they have to be open about who will receive what information and why.

If selective sharing of information is not handled this way, the team members who eventually find that information on the "grapevine" will feel like they are not valued members of the team. This is no way to improve collaboration on project teams.

Partiality

Business Analysts will occasionally have to resolve conflicts or disagreements on teams, but they cannot achieve this objective when they take sides. Partiality or its appearance especially during conflict resolution can seriously damage the spirit of collaboration on a project team.

Some project team members interpret partiality as exclusion or favoritism with the end result that they are not invested in the objectives of the project.

Flexibility and Compromise

If a Business Analyst is uncompromising and inflexible in what they demand from team members, they will likely break the collaborative spirit of that team. Life "happens" to team members; they fall ill, go on vacations, or have to provide care for family members. These unforeseen situations put a lot of stress on team members in addition to their project deliverables. A Business Analyst who demands without compromise that an assignment be achieved come hell or high water is setting themselves up as the destroyer of team collaboration.

What should they do in such instances? Seeking solutions with the Project Manager and the concerned team members would be a good first start; riding roughshod over them though harms team collaboration.

Communication Skills

Actively listening to the concerns of team members is a great start just as ignoring them or partially listening to them will not endear those team members to the Business Analyst or the project objectives.

The same goes for nonverbal cues. Business Analysts who miss body language signals from team members signal a lack of interest in what the team members are communicating nonverbally. To other team members, it may signal a lack of self-awareness, empathy, or interest on the part of the Business Analyst in other project team members, all of which damages the collaborative ethic on the project team.

Conflict Management

Conflict on software development projects is generally considered a dirty word with negative connotations. This may be true depending on where you stand but at its heart if it refers to two or more parties who cannot agree on a position in order to move forward with the process of project delivery. Conflicts arise when project actors cannot agree on project strategy, project objectives, problem definition, solutions, budgets, timelines, end user requirements, and project leadership among a host of many other issues that become flash points for conflicts.

Just like in real life, it's perfectly fine to disagree over issues, and project environments are no different. However, these disagreements become full-blown conflicts when project actors represent entrenched inflexible positions that require intermediaries like Business Analysts to step into and resolve.

The first chapter of this book pointed out that the role of the Business Analyst is that of an intermediary, and conflict management is where this role gets to be played at a deeper level. Business Analysts are largely facilitators in the conflict resolution space during project delivery. Does that mean that Business Analyst don't get into conflicting positions with other project actors? Of course not. They do have conflicts with other project actors, and those methods in use to triage conflicts between different project actors can also be used to triage conflicts that Business Analysts will be involved in.

Why Conflicts Need to Be Brought Under Control on Projects

Stifles Engagement with Project Goals

Project actors fixated on their conflicts and how to win the next round or stalemate the conflict eventually detract from the goals and objectives of the project. Their conflicts take center stage, and project deliverables take a miserable second place (or worse) in the overall scheme of things.

Slows Project Momentum and Erodes Collaboration

Unresolved conflicts damage the spirit and ethic of collaboration during project delivery. End users and stakeholders start to view each other as contestants instead of collaborators, and without collaboration project momentum starts to stall. Project actors also become defined by the conflicts they are engaged in and start to view other project actors with disdain and mistrust. Under these circumstances, it becomes difficult to decide or support a solution without some project actors viewing it through the lens of the conflict they are engaged in.

Entrenches Positions and Opinions

Much like untreated wounds, conflicts will fester and get worse if not brought under control. Conflicting stakeholders or project team members that don't see eye to eye harden their positions or opinions, and unless a resource like a Business Analyst steps in to defuse the conflict, the hardened positions become more entrenched and disruptive

How Conflict Resolution Works and What Business Analysts Can Do to Improve This Skill

It's not something you would wish for your worst enemy, but the more conflicts Business Analysts defuse, the more expertise they garner in the conflict management and resolution space. This is one muscle that mostly grows by application and experience. While other interpersonal skills have clearly laid out avenues by which they can be improved, conflict management is largely improved by taking on and resolving more conflicts. Here's how Business Analysts simultaneously resolve conflicts and grow their conflict resolution muscles as well.

Knowledge of the Issues Causing the Conflict

While Business Analysts are largely facilitators during episodes of conflict resolution, they have to equip themselves with at least some passing knowledge of the issues that project actors are fighting over. Business Analysts can review who the main actors in the conflict are, what they are conflicted about, for how long it has been going on, and whether there have been similar conflicts in the past about the same issues.

Investigating Underlying Issues

A lot of times, the conflicts between stakeholders or those that exist between stakeholders and projects are signs of deeper underlying issues that may even be unrelated to the project. Maybe the end users feel that new processes will displace them and leave them jobless, they may be scared of learning new skills, or they don't believe the project will fix their broken processes or systems. In other instances, the feuds are really about departmental control of resources, influence, and power. For Business Analysts looking to step into conflict resolution, the first touch point is checking what the underlying and unsaid issues are and how long they have been at play. Gaining these deeper insights into the causes of conflict puts the Business Analyst in a better position to get a handle on the conflict and resolve it with finality.

Clarifying Implications of Non-negotiable Positions

During the requiring scoping process or even later stages of the project cycle, conflicts will arise when some project components are considered nonnegotiable.

Take the case of a stakeholder who insists they would like all the data in an older application to be migrated to a new application before the new application can be launched to end users. They go so far as to say that this position is nonnegotiable and demand that the project expressly commits to getting this done. This type of demand has the potential to become an intractable conflict and savvy Business Analysts resolve these types of issues by helping the stakeholder understand their demands and the implications. The Business Analyst could, for example, point out the extra costs involved in migrating and managing more data than is necessary or pointing out how fast the application works when it stores only a few years' worth of data.

Focus on Similarities Instead of Differences

While it may not be prudent to lecture end users and stakeholders about the importance of "oneness" or working together as a team, there are subtle methods that Business Analysts can use that reduce or eliminate siloed thinking. Those same approaches can be applied where "us vs. them" mindsets persist on projects.

As long as the parties in conflict still share the objectives of delivering a functional product, then the conflicts are really about methods and tactics. In a sense they already have more in common than they realize. In the end one product will be delivered, and while there is disagreement on the methods and tactics to get there, it does not mean that the conflicting parties are as different as their conflicts would have them believe.

By focusing on shared objectives, common goals, and points of similarity despite the differences, Business Analysts can reduce demonization of the "other" and create mutual trust, respect, and an understanding of each other's interests. Focusing on similarities rather than differences—even when they genuinely exist—is a more productive conflict management tool over the life span of the project.

Demystifying Sacred Cows

Conflicts by their nature are tinged with egocentrism or self-centeredness. We tend to think we are right, and the other side has no idea what they are doing, and yet they could just as easily say the same thing about us.

One of the key roles of a Business Analyst in a conflict resolution role is to help show the warring parties each other's point of view as well as showing them the upsides and downsides of both sets of views. Demonstrating the strengths and weaknesses of entrenched positions tones down what the parties previously viewed as nonnegotiable sacred cows. This action reduces the aura of self-assuredness and self-centeredness that was the key ingredient in fomenting the conflict in the first place.

While it's difficult to neutralize the egocentrism and self-assuredness that exacerbates conflicts, Business Analysts can demystify these positions and create openings to resolve intractable conflicts by putting the ideas and positions of the egoists under the microscope. The emphasis is to be placed on evaluating the ideas on their own merits with little consideration of how loudly or aggressively an end user or stakeholder pushes those ideas.

Communication Skills

It's pointless for a Business Analysts to step into a conflict resolution role and then not actively listen to the conflicting parties. It's the first stop for a Business Analyst looking to get a grasp of both the underlying and surface issues that are brewing conflicts between different project actors.

In the same boat is the application of role-play borne out of emotional intelligence that allows a Business Analyst to get a feel of how both actors view their side of the conflict.

Equally important is for a Business Analyst to successfully facilitate a safe space so that the conflicting actors can have a meaningful dialogue about the issues roiling them and how they can triage them and move forward with project delivery.

Very early in my Business Analyst career, one of my mentors remarked that the Business Analyst practice was more of people management than actual Business Analysis work. At the time I thought it was a sweeping statement that was probably off the mark. Looking back and based on what I have seen, he wasn't far off the mark, and the need for interpersonal skills demonstrates that point. Without interpersonal skills the management of end users, stakeholders, and project team members is going to difficult, and it eventually impacts that other aspects of a Business Analysts assignments.

Interpersonal skills are a wide subject, and this chapter references those skills that Business Analyst practitioners rely on the most. There are more skills that Business Analysts need to excel at their craft, and one of the key ones is creativity, problem-solving, and analytical thinking to which we turn to next.

Creativity, Problem-Solving, and Strategic Thinking Skills

While software product development teams are resourced by pooling team members with different skillsets and abilities, Business Analysts are placed on teams so that they can tie disparate project strands together.

When requirements are scoped by Business Analysts, they follow them through to deployment, and along the way they inevitably encounter challenges and blockers of varying degrees. These challenges and blockers are removed by Business Analysts flexing their analytical thinking, critical thinking, and problem-solving capabilities.

© Roni Lubwama 2020
R. Lubwama, *The Inside Track to Excelling As a Business Analyst*,
https://doi.org/10.1007/978-1-4842-5543-8_8

Analytical and critical thinking in the context of the Business Analyst practice is the process of decomposing complex data or information and analyzing it to build a case or resolve a problem. It is also the ability to review information by running it through a series of validation scenarios which involve asking questions like

- Is it true?

- What conclusion does the data support?

- Is it a real or an imaginary need?

- What trends do the historical data point to?

- What is the use case?

On the surface it may appear that by exercising this skill Business Analysts, do not trust the information they elicit from end users and stakeholders.

This skill is not about trust or the lack of it; it is about evaluating, analyzing, and interpreting the data, use cases, facts, assumptions, and other factors that are critical for delivering a functional product to end users. It is just another version of "better safe than sorry."

This book will consider the key interpersonal skills that Business Analysts use during the process of project delivery. At a high level, these are the key skills lined up for consideration:

- **Creativity and Problem-Solving Skills**

  This is when Business Analysts come up with solutions and answers to the challenges that plague the software delivery process. This usually done by harnessing the disparate skillsets of project actors and working in concert with the wider project team.

- **Decision-Making**

  Business Analysts in the process of solving problems and developing solutions have to make decisions given the available information and prevailing circumstances. This skill also considers how Business Analysts can get a grip on indecision.

- **Strategic Thinking and Visioning**

  This refers to when Business Analysts envision project deliverables in terms of their day to day deliverables. In effect they take the long-term view of a project and how they can sustain its momentum based on what they are doing at that particular moment.

- **Managing Ambiguity**

   The lack of clarity and structure on projects breeds ambiguity. Managing ambiguity by providing clarity where none exists is a key skill for Business Analysts.

- **Analytical and Critical Thinking Skills**

   When Business Analysts think through requirements, the downstream impacts of decisions and the interconnectedness of disparate software product components are the essence of thinking analytically and critically about project deliverables.

Creativity and Problem-Solving Skills

If you want to understand how this skill is vital to Business Analyst excellence, peruse any posting for a Business Analyst role and chances, are there will be a bullet point for "needs to be creative and a problem-solver."

Projects and organizations will pay a pretty penny for Business Analysts who can demonstrate sizeable problem-solving muscles. Projects are afflicted by problems small and big, and there is no telling when a problem will come calling. The people who hire Business Analysts are not just hiring a person who can dazzle with business analysis skills but a resource who can studiously and methodically review a problem and figure out to quickly get it resolved.

The reality is project leadership (sponsors and managers) is not interested in hearing the problems afflicting a project; they already know those problems, and if they don't, they will know them soon enough.

Their expectation is that the Business Analyst will only be talking about the problems and about how they will quickly make those problems disappear. In effect they expect the Business Analyst to be running toward the fire and quickly put it out, not just narrate how hot or colorful it is.

A Business Analyst who builds a track record of putting out fires is going to be in high demand given the challenges that plague software development projects today.

What sort of problems can a Business Analyst expect to encounter on projects?

- End users and stakeholders who repeatedly shift boundaries on requirements. What they requested yesterday in no longer required the next day. There is a reason why the refrain *"they don't know what they want"* is a popular staple on software development projects.

- Technical limitations of software products that lead to the delivery of software products that do not fully meet end user requirements or expectations.

- Teams external to the project team that do not deliver what is expected from them on time leading to delays.

- Missed requirements late into the product development cycle.

- Lack of experienced project team members and lack of experience implementing new technologies.

These are just examples of blockers that Business Analysts are expected to remove and get the project back on track, but there are many more hairy ones that if not triaged effectively can seriously impede project progress.

How Do Business Analysts Solve These Problems?

The answer makes solid material for another book, but at a high level, they can use a combination of non-technical and technical skills to resolve problems.

There are also frameworks like the 5 Whys, RCA (Root Cause Analysis), Means–End Analysis, Ideation and many more that Business Analysts can also use to triage problems especially the types that keep recurring.

For our purposes we will review how Business Analysts resolve problems using creativity in the context of software development projects. Here's how that can be done.

Evaluating the Facts and Data

Getting the information, data, and facts pertaining to a problem is of critical importance if Business Analysts are going to solve any problems.

It is of crucial importance to analyze the facts and data before choosing a course of action when seeking solutions to a problem. Informed problem-solving not only provides the guardrails that prevent the deployment of inadequate solutions but also prevents those solutions from worsening the problem.

This does not mean taking longer than is necessary to resolve an issue because the Business Analyst is still "researching" the problem; rather it relates to obtaining the key facts and seeking a speedy solution based on available information and data.

Working in Concert with the Project Team

This may seem counterintuitive given that we just stated that Business Analysts should be pumped up to personally resolve problems. The best Business Analysts don't have to have all the answers to the problems in front of them, but what they are good at is knowing *who* has the answers or solutions they need.

They realize that project teams have a mix of team members with diverse sets of skillsets as well as experiences and that in crisis situations they can leverage those skillsets and experiences to beat back problems.

Creativity helps Business Analysts figure out the best resource or means to resolve a problem in the shortest time while also minimizing possible risks that are likely to arise from the solution.

Acting with Urgency

If a Business Analyst got word of a problem last month, why are they picking it up for resolution a month later?

This is hypothetical, but the wider point is that ace Business Analysts act with urgency when they are faced with a problem that stalls or is likely to stall project progress.

This is not to say Business Analysts should just dive in like headless chickens in seeking issue resolution; facts ought to be collected, and a course of action set in as short a time as can be reasonable.

And no, a 30-day lead time for acting is unacceptable.

Why Are Problem-Solving Abilities Important to Projects?

Problem-Solving Keeps Projects on Track

A software development project in some ways (but not literally) can be compared to being in the trenches of a pitched battle with projectiles flying in all directions.

While some projects are well-organized and run smoothly, those tend to be the exceptions; most projects are going to be bedeviled by multifaceted problems of varying magnitudes.

Planning for eventualities does help, but it's not a foolproof insurance policy against project gremlins. However, a project that enlists a creative and methodical problem-solver as a Business Analyst also acquires an insurance policy that will own and resolve those problems.

That insurance policy by way of a problem busting Business Analyst is the one that corrals the resources and brains necessary to remove the blockers and problems stalling project progress.

Improves the Knowledge Base

Solving problems provides Business Analysts with the expertise and knowledge they need to resolve similar problems should they arise in the future. Without problem-solving there is not much learning or new knowledge gained for either the project or the Business Analyst.

Fosters Transparency and Communication

Ever tried hiding a candle in the dark? Same analogy applies to diagnosing and attempting to resolve problems without openness or transparency. If a project component is troubled, the first course of action would be to inform the wider project team and depending on the severity inform stakeholders as well.

In other words, bring the problem out in the open where help can be sought and more brains can be brought to bear on the problem so as to get a quick resolution.

Suppressing information about problems can turn a minor spark into a major blaze with unpredictable outcomes later in the project cycle.

Needless to say, it's also unprofessional not to flag problems as they arise.

How Can Business Analysts Improve Their Problem-Solving Skills?

Active Listening

This is a big one.

A Business Analyst who does not carefully listen is likely to either solve the wrong problem or solve nothing at all. Active listening is the first line of defense in the problem-solving process, and Business Analysts who underrate it are courting trouble.

Problem Identification

This is a difficult skill to master as it grows the more problems a Business Analysts solves, but at its heart, it refers to checking if there is clarity of thought that identifies the problem.

What strategies are in place for locking down the source of the problem or why is there a recurrence of the problem? Those types of questions are essential for identifying the "problem behind the problem" well before laying down strategies to resolve the problem.

Clarity of the problem is way more important than how to solve it or which tools to deploy toward problem resolution.

Downplaying Confirmation Bias

A Business Analyst who always uses a hammer to solve problems comes to view every problem as a nail. Confirmation bias refers to using data or selecting solutions that confirm one's personal biases—in other words, it is the viewing of every problem as a nail when you have a hammer. The thinking is that if the data or solutions don't conform to a Business Analyst's worldview, then the data or solutions are not part of the problem-solving process.

Removing confirmation bias when evaluating data and solutions to problems gives Business Analysts the opportunity to consider a wide range of conclusions from the data as well as alternative solutions to problems.

Being Open-Minded

Closely following on confirmation bias is the tendency to be close-minded or narrow-minded. It's a different take on confirmation bias.

Business Analysts who have solved a problem a certain way in the past are closed to new and better options to solve the same problem. Sometimes it is encouraged by the attitude; "that's how we have always done it here."

Creative problem-solving requires open and flexible minds as well minds that consider different perspectives.

Groupthink

Ever been in a room where the audience does not want to disagree with the boss out of deference, fear, intimidation, or conflict avoidance? It happens, and it also happens to be one of the worst ways to resolve problems.

The boss thinks they have the best idea, but without questioning or validating the idea, how else can anyone say with conviction that it is the best idea on the table?

Groupthink may reduce the likelihood of conflicts or ensure that there is forward motion, but it stunts the creative process and consideration of alternative solutions.

Decision-Making

Do Business Analysts have to make critical decisions on projects? Yes, they do, and sometimes they put off making those decisions until circumstances force their hand. Business Analysts are normally required to make decisions when a progress-blocking problem requires an urgent solution or when a critical decision needs to be made and communicated immediately.

A good example is when a Business Analyst puts off the decision to inform stakeholders and end users that they are not getting all the bells and whistles they asked for during the requirements scoping process. What usually happens is that the technical team will inform the Business Analyst that there is a technical limitation that will prevent the delivery of the said bells and whistles requested by end users.

An update of this nature will typically require updating the scope of work and engaging in negotiations with end users to define what they will accept as a functional software product. But for this to happen, the Business Analyst needs to pull the trigger and immediately inform end users. Putting off this action becomes indecision or the lack of a decision, and for as long as end users are in the dark about this decision, then they are technically being "strung along" by the Business Analyst.

The best Business Analysts simply collect the facts or data, chart a negotiation course, make the decision to inform end users, and inform them regardless of the consequences. Will it be painful? Maybe or maybe not; it depends on how invested the end users are in the components they will not be receiving. Worst-case scenario is that end users will ask project management or organizational leadership to get involved in this decision.

At the end of the day, there is no compelling reason to sit on a decision of this magnitude. Business Analysts need to get the relevant facts or data that support a decision, evaluate that data, analyze likely risks, and make the decision.

But why would Business Analysts be indecisive?

- If the project or organization runs on a culture of fear or avoiding "looking bad," then that culture breeds indecision from Business Analysts.

- Allied to the above is the politics of who makes decisions. If there is a history of decisions being taken and then reversed the following day, that does not augur well, and the Business Analyst will adopt a wait-and-see attitude when decisions need to be taken.

- Maybe they don't have all the information and they are waiting for critical information that will help them defend the decision during negotiations with end users.

- Sometimes they assume the end users already know. This one is dicey, and it is best practice to confirm with end users if information pertaining to the decision has already reached them.

- It may also be that the Business Analyst is waiting for the perfect time or "mood" to relay the decision especially if there is a likelihood of the situation getting ugly once they have made the decision and communicated it.

Why Decision-Making Is Important for Business Analysts on Projects

Keeps Project Actors on the Same Page

In the previous hypothetical scenario where the Business Analyst was indecisive, the Business Analyst might be aware of the technical limitation but does not convey the information to end users who are ultimately the customers of the project. Making decisions and communicating those decisions (whether good or bad) keeps end users, stakeholders, and project team members on the same page.

Keeps Projects in Motion

Making decisions and standing by them keeps projects in motion, while sitting on decisions creates inertia. When decisions are made, it has cascading effects on the components and actors of the project who are relying on this decision. Without this decision, there is inertia and slowed project motion.

Resolves Sticky Problems

This is an obvious one.

Problems, challenges, and blockers don't disappear by themselves; that would be too easy. Someone, usually a Business Analyst, must make the hard decisions that expunges problems, challenges, and blockers. The alternative is also true; when Business Analysts don't make the decisions that resolve problems, then those problems start to fester and become more difficult to resolve by the day.

Builds Trust and Credibility

When a Business Analyst reaches out to stakeholders and end users with a difficult decision they made, stakeholders can see that the Business Analyst is making an effort at resolving their pain points. It may have been the wrong decision and probably didn't work either, but they will appreciate the effort. This action-oriented attitude builds trust and credibility with end users and stakeholders.

Builds and Maintains Relationships

Another obvious one and closely following on how Business Analysts build credibility is by making the hard calls. End users, stakeholders, and project team members will be well disposed to have a great relationship with a Business Analyst who is making the tough calls on their behalf. Likewise, they won't be well disposed to a Business Analyst who does not treat their pain points urgently going by the glacial pace at which decisions are made and communicated.

How Can Business Analysts Improve Decision-Making?

Manage Analysis Paralysis

This is when overanalyzing and overthinking a problem eventually creates paralysis, and the problem does not get resolved. Analysis paralysis occurs when a Business Analyst tries to collate and analyze *all* the information or data regarding an issue or problem. Of course, in the real world, Business Analysts cannot get and evaluate in a timely fashion all the information pertaining to a problem. What is required are the key facts, consensus, and flexibility as the solution is implemented.

Plug Key Information Gaps

This is the opposite of analysis paralysis, and it is where a decision is taken with scanty or incomplete information. As mentioned, it's impossible to have all the required information, but it is also ideal to have the key pieces of information before pulling the trigger on a decision.

Focusing on the Trees Instead of the Forest

Focusing on small insignificant details or obsessing over the odds of a failure of a decision also contributes to situations where Business Analysts sit on decisions or are afraid of taking decisions. It takes the focus away from the long-term project objectives (the forest) and focuses on the trivial details (trees) of a situation.

Can a Business Analyst be 100% sure that the decision that has been made will be successful? Not unless they are into fortune-telling. Obsessing over minute details or the success odds of a decision is a waste of time. This time is better spent figuring out how to improve the odds of success or taking the actions that will ensure that the decision is successful.

Removing Emotions and Fear from the Decision

The emotions a Business Analyst carries into the decision-making process can either make or break the decisions. The fear that a decision will be a colossal failure can create indecisiveness just as the fear of "looking bad" will achieve the same result.

In order to make better and informed decisions with greater chances of success, Business Analysts need to do their best to remove negative emotions from this process. Positive emotions like overconfidence can be just as destructive to this process as it can lead to glossing over risks and potential pitfalls.

As human beings we want to be emotionally involved in the decisions we make, and this is acceptable. What is unacceptable is letting emotions drive the decision-making process for Business Analysts.

Managing the Sunk Cost Fallacy

Sunk costs refer to expenses that have been made that are irrecoverable regardless of the size of the investment. As humans we, for example, rationalize that we don't want to give up on a business because we have already spent so much time, effort, and money on it. To economists what has already been spent is an irrecoverable sunk cost done in the past and should not determine decisions that the business owner needs to make today.

To make better decisions, Business Analysts need to be wary of the sunk cost's fallacy. Business Analysts can compare how decisions were made in the past as well as outcomes, but past decisions regardless of their outcomes should not scuttle decisions that need to be made in the moment.

Strategic Thinking and Visioning

The requirements scoping process, supporting the technical process of software product development, and unplugging the blockers that plague software projects are the tactical deliverables expected from Business Analysts on a day to day basis.

Put together these tactical milestones and components are what comprise the overall bigger picture of the project objectives. Strategic visioning and thinking then are concerned with project deliverables in the context of what the Business Analyst and project environment deliver at a tactical level on a day to day basis. Strategic thinking reviews the actions taking place in a project environment today and evaluates the benefits, potential impacts, and risks to the vision that the projects seek to deliver tomorrow.

I have heard it said on projects that Business Analysts have no say in strategic matters pertaining to a project, for example, which technical solutions should be implemented and why or which business process needs to be reengineered and why. That is true to an extent, but it's also true that the definition of the strategic value a Business Analyst brings to a project has changed over time.

It is no longer just the remit of Business Analysts to manage requirements and how they are delivered; there are other inputs that they are charged with delivering that very much require strategic visioning and thinking.

What Does Strategic Thinking and Visioning Look Like for Business Analysts?

Project Lifespan Planning

This is not so much as forward planning that plans so many years into the future but more like a strategic roadmap that focuses on the overall lifespan of the project. Can all the requirements be delivered in the stipulated time frame? Can the project move through the entire Software Development Life Cycle in the 6 months that the Project Sponsors will fund? What happens if the project is incomplete in that 6-month period? These are the types of questions that a Business Analyst will strategically think about where the lifespan of a project is concerned.

Risk Assessment and Mitigation

Working in concert with Project Managers, Business Analysts review risks that are likely to derail or slow project delivery. More importantly they can work with end users, stakeholders, and project team members to mitigate those risks.

Closely allied to risk management is scenario building in concert with project leadership that reviews worst and best case scenarios and what that means for project delivery.

Aligning Project Goals with Organizational Goals

This refers to applying strategic thinking to end user requirements by challenging requirements, use cases, and assumptions that appear to defeat organizational goals and objectives.

How Business Analysts Use Strategic Thinking to Deliver Projects

Tactical Challenges and Their Impacts on Project Goals

Consider delays arising from changes to the scope by end users and stakeholders. Changes to scope may look like manageable impacts to a project, but more often than not, if not managed properly, they lead to costly project extensions. This is because the project is taking on more work than it initially committed to, and extending the project by even a few days has financial and resource implications.

A Business Analyst faced with problems like proposed scope changes or indecisive stakeholders relies on strategic thinking to evaluate what these tactical challenges mean for the longer-term objective of delivering a functional software product.

Evaluating Requirements for Future Environments

End users and stakeholders more often than not are more concerned with how a pain point they have today can be quickly resolved. When requests are made for new or improved software products, the focus of end users is not so much as what happens a year or two from now but how quickly a pain point is eliminated today.

Who can blame them? They are the frontline soldiers who have to deal with angry customers, declining sales revenue, and all the nastiness emanating from unpredictable market environments. Thinking about the future be damned!

In the current business environment, strategically thinking about the future in terms of the end user requirements requested today is a role that has largely been outsourced to Business Analysts and other project members like technical architects.

Upon receiving requirements, Business Analysts need to review if the ask is compatible with the long-term goals and objectives of the organization. End users who, for example, request software products based on current usage need to be asked about scalability. They need to be challenged about whether they have considered the fact that the product they requested cannot scale, and it certainly cannot handle the rapid business growth that the organization is targeting.

This is the essence of strategic visioning and thinking at the requirements scoping level.

How Can Business Analysts Improve Their Strategic Thinking Skills?

Embrace Strategic Thinking As a Mindset

This refers to inculcating a mindset that considers the long term for any tactical actions that are undertaken during the project delivery process. Will the solution meet end user requirements a few years from now? How can end user adoption and ease of product use be incorporated in the delivered product so that end users will easily and quickly adopt the product now and in the future?

Growing this mindset is easier said than done, but with exposure to more project environments especially those that didn't turn out so well, Business Analysts can grow this mindset. It also develops when it is nurtured as a habit and treated as an ongoing process during the project delivery process.

Using an Entrepreneurial Mindset

Entrepreneurs are in the business of creating solutions and efficiencies where none currently exist. Does a solution eliminate a complex problem while adding more value? Will the solution do it efficiently and save money and other resources? Are there cheaper and more efficient alternatives? There are many more questions that an entrepreneur can ask in the pursuit of efficient solutions.

The Business Analyst practice is no different, and the best Business Analysts in the business will be asking the same if not similar questions during the project delivery process.

Granted Business Analysts don't count the pennies on a project or determine the overall strategy a project follows, but by their daily tactical actions, they can meaningfully contribute to a project by asking questions of strategic import like

- Will this change in scope lead to costly and lengthy delays?

- How can we help end users resolve their pain points so that they can be more efficient or profitable?

- How can the implementation of this solution help the stakeholders' organization be more competitive in their marketplaces?

Business Analysts who deploy this mindset are not only thinking like entrepreneurs, but they are also using strategic thinking to flag inefficiencies inherent in the project delivery process.

Managing Ambiguity

Ambiguity refers to dealing with complex, vague, undefined, information-deficient concepts, situations, and environments. Ambiguity is inherent in the change management process because the process works with many unknowns in highly complex and fluid business environments.

This is not hyperbole, but projects hire Business Analysts so that they can make sense of unstructured information, evaluate that information, and bring order to end user requirements and project deliverables. In a roundabout way, Business Analysts are assigned to projects so that they can reduce ambiguity by ordering the unordered and structuring the unstructured.

A key thing about ambiguity is that it cannot be fully eliminated, but it can be largely reduced so that the process of project delivery moves forward with structured deliverables and objectives.

What Does Ambiguity Look Like for Business Analysts?

Unstructured and Undefined Requirements

Anyone who has held a Business Analyst position for even a day can relate to this situation. Requirements are unclear, and in many cases, they have more than one interpretation. End users and stakeholders think they know what they need until Business Analysts start asking questions, and from the answers, it becomes clear end users are not sure what they need. At other times the end users know what they need, they are just having a hard time articulating that need. This lack of articulation is not helped by shifting boundaries of what end users classify as a functional product. The laundry list of these situations is never ending, but this is precisely how ambiguity is created and manifested.

Lack of Documented Processes

Many organizations have business processes and workflows that are "documented" only in the minds of certain end users. There is scanty documentation that details how those processes work or how they are used. As long as the organization is meeting its objectives, this is largely acceptable until, that is, requirements need to be scoped. End users cannot agree on how workflows and processes actually work, why they work differently from how they were designed, and what triggered those changes. When Business Analysts start eliciting requirements, they find that requirements are open to many interpretations and impacts. What is obvious to end users is not so obvious to Business Analysts, so those unstated requirements become missed requirements. This lack of structure and process disorientation is the true definition of ambiguity.

Poor Communication and Information Gaps

An organizational culture that prizes the hoarding of information is certain to infect projects with ambiguity. With scanty information, some project actors' resort to guessing or hypothesizing as a way of plugging the information gaps. This is akin to walking in the dark, and it is certain to worsen ambiguity.

Related to information gaps is poor communication modes where critical information is couched in techiy jargon or "corporate lingo" that masks the real meaning behind the communication.

Fear of Failure

How does an organization treat failure? Is it a hammer and tongs or a learn from the experience approach? Much like indecision, the fear of failure causes project actors including Business Analysts to be extra cautious during project delivery for they are not sure whether they are going be flamed or lionized whichever direction they take. One minute they are confident about a course of action, and the next minute they trash the plan as there are "indications" that project sponsors are unhappy with the plan even though they won't say so explicitly. This second-guessing and "mind reading" breeds ambiguity.

How Can Business Analysts Improve Their Ambiguity Reduction and Management Skills?

Acceptance of Ambiguity

Most people live their lives with structure and habits that help them navigate the different demands and challenges they face. We are also taught from childhood that if we are going to be successful in life, we have to live structured lives. It therefore comes as a shocker to many Business Analysts when they realize that while software development projects have structures on paper, the reality is that many times project delivery is going to be an unstructured maze. They discover that there is a lot of ambiguity and gray areas in the project delivery process.

One key to the management of ambiguity is to grow a mindset that accepts ambiguity as part of the software product development process. These questions illustrate this point succinctly: Will Business Analysts have all the answers to the various challenges that arise during project delivery? Very unlikely. Will Business Analysts miss requirements? Definitely. Assuming that they somehow had all the answers they needed, is there a guarantee that the solutions deployed will be successful? Nope!

Accepting that ambiguity is a part of software project delivery is the first step toward managing and reducing ambiguity. Well, that attitude is defeatist you say; it isn't, and I will accept that it's defeatist when I start seeing projects delivered free of ambiguity.

Identify the Known Quantities

If the requirements scoping process is plagued by information black holes and gray areas, Business Analysts can plug them by identifying what they *do know*. Once they collate the available information, the next step of identifying the missing information while still challenging becomes more manageable. Sometimes it turns out that the unknown information has very little bearing on the proposed solutions and that the available information is enough to move forward with problem resolution. Coloring the part of the information black hole as a known quantity is effective in ambiguity reduction.

Quit the Waffling

As stated previously, fear and the absence of direction create ambiguity and even worse leads to indecision or waffling. This can be combated when Business Analysts boldly and directly communicate the course of action as well as being transparent about the ambiguity surrounding the decision. Put another way, by putting their plan out there to end users, stakeholders, and project team members, Business Analysts are inviting help that improves their ideas and fleshes out the ambiguity as well.

The best Business Analysts start by asking, "what is the worst that could happen?" and just run with the ball with the available information plus a dash of confidence. Ambiguity is not one to be beaten with indecision and a lack of confidence.

Effective Communication

Clearly communicating intention regardless of the communication channel used helps reduce ambiguity. Concise emails and presentations that use language tailored to the audience can reduce ambiguity where it exists. The use of technical jargon or unnecessarily complex grammar and vocabulary does little to reduce ambiguity; if anything, these actions are likely to intensify ambiguity. The use of nonverbal cues also helps Business Analysts gauge whether an audience is clear-eyed on what needs to be done or whether the presentation has created more confusion and ambiguity.

Process Flexibility

As they go about the project delivery process, Business Analysts can be sticklers for process, structure, and convention. In extreme cases, they trust the processes so much that they become hostages to these strictures. A good example is when Business Analysts want to always work through a structured requirements elicitation process as they scope requirements on software projects. But what happens when the end users cannot define their requirements and don't know what the end product should look like or what it should do for them? Does this mean that the requirements elicitation process is dead at that point? Of course not; it just means that the Business Analyst has to embrace methods that can handle such vague and ambiguous situations.

This scenario is the true definition of ambiguity, and it cannot be resolved by Business Analysts who typically use a "one size fits all" approach for requirements elicitation.

The other aspect of flexibility refers to the ability to literally "turn on a dime" as and when new information becomes available depending on the challenge or problem that is being resolved. The reality is Business Analysts solve problems without all the important information which causes even more ambiguity about outcomes. The readiness to course-correct as conditions and circumstances change is one way to reduce ambiguity.

End User Collaboration

Requirements ambiguity causing nail-biters? Business Analysts can opt for the oldest trick in the book—engage with more end users to gain more insights and information. The more information and data that is collated and evaluated, the more likely that the Business Analysts will start to see previously unrecognized patterns and trends that provide structure to requirements. In general terms the more brain power that is enlisted to clarify vague concepts, the more likely it is that more facts and information useful to the requirements scoping process will be brought to light. Old school requirements scoping techniques like job shadowing are very effective in ambiguity reduction as they clarify vague concepts in real time.

Visualizing Information

Sometimes end users and stakeholders cannot accurately articulate what a software product or business process should do for them or what pain points it will resolve. In those instances, laying out current processes visually by using process maps, use cases, mock-ups, and prototypes clarifies end user needs and assumptions as well as exposing the risks inherent in both the current and proposed solutions.

Visualization goes a long way in reducing ambiguity especially around the requirements scoping process, and the best Business Analysts when faced with a lot of ambiguity use more of visualization than verbalization.

Using Agile or Scrum Software Development Methodology

Without doubt, the development of the Agile/Scrum methodology was targeted at the management of ambiguity on software development projects. By using an iterative process of software development for project delivery, the Agile methodology essentially accepts the fact that projects will be plagued by uncertainty and ambiguity. If end users and stakeholders keep coming up with new requirements, it's probably because their processes are undefined or they are at the mercy of external push and pull factors that demand these changes.

End users and stakeholders without accurately defined or shifting requirements cause a lot of requirements ambiguity which is best managed by using an iterative software development methodology like Agile. If end users are unsure what a product should do, developing a prototype and showing it to them clarifies their needs and forms the basis for the next round of require-ments scoping and actual product development.

By trusting the Agile methodology, Business Analysts can get a handle on the ambiguity hovering over the requirements scoping process and the wider project delivery process.

Analytical and Critical Thinking Skills

Analytical and critical thinking abilities are at their most basic powers of logi-cal thinking, situational analysis, and reasoning abilities for Business Analysts. These powers enable Business Analysts to apply critiques and logical reason-ing to requirements scoping, project challenges, project blockers, or any other situation that needs triaging in order to move forward with project delivery.

While time is of the essence on projects, Business Analysts must nevertheless apply analytical and critical thinking to the issues, challenges, and situations that they encounter on projects. Additionally, While data analysis is impor-tant to elicit patterns from data, analytical thinking is an all-encompassing capability that considers many more variables than just data analysis. Business Analysts are regularly asked to resolve challenges that are far removed from data analysis but which require the brain power of analytical and critical thinking skills. Decision-making is one of those activities that Business Analysts have to carefully think through after evaluating the data, likely impacts of the decision, and the effect of the decision on extraneous factors like other organizational departments.

Analytical and critical thinking is also not to be confused with merely being overly critical of other project actors or their ideas, and it is certainly not the same as being argumentative. It should also not be looked at as the processing of information that is required to enable the day to day activities of a Business Analyst. It is much more than that, and its application generates the type of ideas and concepts that unlock problems, resolve challenges, improve requirements, and provide clarity to end user and stakeholder use cases.

What Does Analytical and Critical Thinking Look Like for Business Analysts?

Understanding Interconnectedness and Dependencies

This refers to reviewing how different systems and processes are interconnected to each other before the process of change is undertaken.

An analytical Business Analyst will build mental models of system or process interconnectedness, and those mental validations will be manifested in the questions they ask end users during the requirements scoping process.

The mental scenario building borne of the critical and analytical thinking process of a Business Analyst will be demonstrated in questions such as

- If we shut down a legacy application for end users A, how about end users B and C who use it more heavily than A end users?

- If that is the case, shouldn't end users B and C be the drivers of change as they will be the most impacted by phasing out the legacy application?

- How come end users A are the advocates for change yet they have the least contact with the application?

These sample mental scenarios are what Business Analysts use to understand how processes are interconnected or dependent upon each other.

Moving these validations from the mind of a Business Analyst to requirements scoping sessions is the next logical step, but for this to happen, the heavy lifting of analytical and critical thinking needs to have taken place first.

Assumption Testing and Validation

This is especially the case with implementing new software products when unverified assumptions can go unchallenged as the project moves toward the final stages of delivery.

Consider a scenario where project sponsors state that they expect at least 90% of end users to adopt the new software product within 1 month of launch or deployment. Without proof to support this assertion, it becomes an assumption, and the critical thinking abilities of Business Analysts kick in by checking the following:

- How is the 90% adoption rate arrived at? Is there a historical record to support this assumption?

- How successful has the organization been with achieving these adoption numbers with other applications for the same set of users in the past?

- How can this assumption be tested or verified before it is accepted?

The Business Analyst by playing devil's advocate—it's not that they don't trust the assumption—is asking valid questions that can stave off future choke points simply because nobody bothered to do assumption testing.

Back to the product adoption scenario.

The Business Analyst checks the data for previous application adoption by the organization and discovers that it hovers in the 40%–50% range; there is no historical record of a 90% adoption rate. Analytical and critical thinking have blown the cover of this assumption so to speak.

This is a good thing (unless you are the project sponsor) for the Business Analyst can now work with the project team and project sponsors to ensure that they deliver the targeted 90% adoption rates.

Essentially the Business Analyst by going through this analytical process and validating the adoption assumptions has increased the odds of the adoption target being achieved. Validating this scenario would not be possible without the magical powers of assumption testing.

Requirements Validation

This is an obvious one as Business Analysts rely on analytical and critical thinking abilities to test the different scenarios resulting from end user requirements.

Consider a Business Analyst who gets a request to scope requirements for phasing out an application with the main complaint being that it takes too long to process large datasets. Wearing the hat of analytical and critical thinking a Business Analyst will ask these and many more questions of end users:

- Who is experiencing the issue and for how long?

- When was it first documented? Why is it being flagged now?

- Is this the purpose (large dataset analysis) for which the application was initially procured?

- Is this a real problem or the intention is to just get rid of the application in exchange for one with more bells and whistles?

End users are usually so focused on eliminating a pain point that they will go so far as requesting a Business Analyst to work toward implementing a specific solution. In those instances (and they do happen), the critical Business Analyst will check the following with end users and stakeholders:

- Why product A and not product B?

- How was this decision arrived at?

- Who sanctioned the decision and why?

These may seem like pedestrian questions, but by verbalizing them, they have the unintended effect of exposing other scenarios and assumptions that need to be investigated in order to build a more coherent case for change. It's more about the thinking process and its outcomes than about what is being asked for.

Also, as previously mentioned, it's not that the Business Analyst does not trust end users or stakeholders; it's in the interest of the Business Analyst to build a defendable watertight case for change, a case that at a minimum has validated key assumptions, scenarios, use cases, and facts.

The Importance of Analytical and Critical Thinking Skills During Product Delivery

Uncovers Hidden Use Cases

By thinking through a process as it was designed and how it works, Business Analysts can uncover hidden use cases and assumptions that may easily go under the radar during requirements discovery sessions.

A good example is when end users get so much trouble using a process that they repurpose it to work differently to achieve the same result. While they have "hacked" or "short-circuited" the process, the reality is that this cool trick does not exist in any manual and resides only in the minds of end users.

The Business Analyst seeking to change this process will need to analyze and consider the process as it was meant to work and how it has been repurposed and incorporate these scenarios in the requirements scoping process.

Analytical and critical thinking are some of the best tools that can be deployed to uncover hidden use cases, assumptions, and scenarios.

Improves Situational Interpretation

Giving an unfolding situation deep thought will equip a Business Analyst with the powers of perspective and analysis in order to accurately interpret what is happening.

That hostile or near-aggressive stakeholder or end user is probably just frustrated and just wants their problems gone; they have nothing against the Business Analyst. What is itching them is the glacial pace of change that makes their workdays miserable as hell.

Prevents Expensive Surprises

Is a Business Analyst procrastinating about a festering blocker, or are they thinking through the ways that blocker can be put to pasture?

We all know what happens to festering blockers if they are left unattended for even a short period of time; they get worse. It's the same analogy with a Business Analyst who by omission or commission does not think through an issue especially around requirements that leads to expensive mistakes down the project cycle.

Motivates and Drives More Analysis

Uncovering likely pitfalls lurking about and pointing them out before they become major issues gets everyone on the same page and spurs even more critical analyses of other requirements that are being proposed.

Asking uncomfortable questions gets end users and stakeholders to think through the requirements and changes they are proposing to Business Analysts.

For Business Analysts critical thinking is a gateway to generating more ideas and concepts that can be used to improve requirements and triage difficult challenges.

How Can Business Analysts Improve Their Critical and Analytical Thinking skills?

Here are a few ways Business Analysts can improve their critical and analytical thinking abilities.

Deploying Communication Skills

Critical and analytical thinking is triggered by information flowing to the Business Analyst, and these triggers are set off when a Business Analyst takes the time to actively listen to end users or stakeholders. Without engaging end users or stakeholders by asking questions and actively listening to them about proposed changes, critical and analytical thinking has no inputs to work with, and the critical abilities of the Business Analyst cannot be fully utilized.

It is also important to use the full suite of communication skills in order to fully develop the analytical and critical thinking muscle. Role-playing which is related to empathy is a particularly good tool for analytical and critical thinking as it allows a Business Analyst to think of ideas and concepts through the "eyes" or lenses of other project actors. This prompts thinking that generates questions like

- What is the motivation of project actors to think and act in a given manner?

- What are the key drivers of their actions and decisions?

- What would I do if I were in "their shoes"?

This role-playing enables Business Analysts to view an issue or challenge from different perspectives which generates the ideas and concepts that are required to improve requirements and resolve challenges during project delivery.

Use of Unconventional Information Sources

Critically evaluating a situation, challenge, or project blocker requires assessing lots of information from different sources. Sometimes what is required especially when solutions are difficult to come by is reviewing how other projects and organizations have resolved a similar challenge. This will usually involve reviewing data or information that is external to the project but which can provide insightful parallels that can generate new ideas for resolving intractable challenges.

Process Mapping

Using visualization tools like process maps to highlight how different business systems or applications work together gives Business Analysts the opportunity to lay out entire processes and expose even the most minute or hidden processes.

By simply reviewing a process map, a Business Analyst can critique an entire process in one view and thereby unearth hidden processes as well as validate use cases inherent in the process map.

Process mapping has the added benefit of bringing to light underlying or unstated assumptions that can distort the requirements scoping process if they are not brought out in the open early in the project cycle.

Staying Open-Minded

Analytical and critical thinking is improved by reviewing the information that is received as it is without bias or judgement. The times when requirements are being submitted by end users is a time to actively listen and ask probing questions. The time to decide when a requirement is superfluous or "nice to have" will come later when the facts, data, and use cases have been analyzed and critiqued on their merits.

Some may opine that this is a waste of everyone's time by eliciting requirements that will not be worked on and that may be true to a point. What is more important is to figure out how end user requirements fit into the overall objectives of the project delivery process.

Self-awareness of the biases of a Business Analyst does improve the process of analytical and creative thinking. During the process of idea conception, Business Analysts have to be conscious whether they are merely copy-pasting another idea or if they are being too confident in a solution. They also need to be conscious of being plagued by the "sunken costs fallacy" (see section on Decision-Making) that focuses on past irrecoverable sunk costs instead of analytically assessing the present situation on its merits.

Collaboration

Analytical and critical thinking abilities are best harnessed by working in concert with other team members and using them as sounding boards for the ideas and concepts that a Business Analyst has developed. By having their ideas critiqued before they are circulated to other project actors, Business Analysts get the opportunity to think through their ideas and further refine them. The refining of ideas and concepts cannot take place when Business Analysts are unwilling to place those ideas under the microscope that is analytical examination. It's one of the best ways for Business Analysts to grow better ideas and concepts.

Critical and analytical thinking skills are important skills that a Business Analyst uses to cut through the unstructured maze that the project environment can sometimes resemble. With creativity, critical thinking, and analytical skills, Business Analysts can make decisions and judgment calls that have wide-reaching impacts on different project components as well as overall project delivery.

For now though we consider a couple of unconventional non-technical skills that are just as critical as the conventional non-technical skills that have just been reviewed by this chapter and the preceding chapters.

Business Analyst Practice Hacks

With technology landscapes that are constantly changing and the fluid demands of customers and stakeholders alike, as a Business Analyst, one can feel at sea amidst these conflicting demands and challenges. In a word there are high expectations despite the myriad challenges strewn about waiting to snare unsuspecting projects and the Business Analysts driving them. There will be moments when these complex challenges, fluid business environments, and equally fluid organizational actors nullify whatever non-technical skill a Business Analyst deploys.

So what does a Business Analyst do when even the application of the non-technical skills highlighted here only moves the project progress needle only marginally?

There is another category of non-technical skills which are better categorized as "hacks" or "workarounds" that can also be used to resolve challenges and remove blockers that plague software development projects. They can be considered as "get out of jail cards," and they get the job of problem resolution done just as well as the conventional non-technical skillsets. How and when they are deployed is up to the Business Analyst, but they are very much part of the Business Analyst survival toolkit.

© Roni Lubwama 2020
R. Lubwama, *The Inside Track to Excelling As a Business Analyst*,
https://doi.org/10.1007/978-1-4842-5543-8_9

Some of these hacks are applied as one-time events, and others have to be consistently applied as long as a Business Analyst is assigned to a project.

Consider some of these hacks.

No Need to Reinvent the Wheel

I have seen this many times on projects that are in motion: a new Business Analyst is hired, and right away they set about compiling new requirements documentation, new process flows, as well as beginning new meetings with project stakeholders.

Unless the Business Analyst being replaced totally bombed the project, I would start by reviewing the documentation compiled by the outgoing Business Analyst however scanty it may be.

It is very likely that the outgoing Business Analyst had done some documentation related to the project and that documentation just needs to be found. In the event that this documentation is unearthed, the Business Analyst can be the judge of whether they want to improve it or dump it altogether though it is more likely that the former option will be more useful.

Building on existing documentation saves truckloads of time by not redoing the documentation that already exists. It also helps Business Analysts with an additional phase of knowledge transfer.

Some organizations have such complex business process that compiling process flows is a time-intensive exercise that also requires the heavy application of analytical abilities to make sense of them. There is no need to get burned out by this stuff especially if a Business Analyst can build on what is already available.

If Business Analysts insist on doing everything anew even when that documentation exists, the one major drawback that is usually encountered is requirements fatigue. If end users have provided the requirements many times over to the Business Analyst's predecessors, then the Business Analyst who insists on eliciting the same requirements from the same end users and stakeholders is unlikely to be well-received. The Business Analyst shouldn't imagine that because end users want changes like yesterday, they also want to spend their days providing the same requirements feedback many times over.

This is one of the worst possible ways a Business Analyst can get started with end users whose goodwill they will need during the entire project delivery process. Sometimes end users don't cooperate during requirements elicitation sessions because they have done it many times before, but they don't see any progress in resolving their pain points.

What they are, however, seeing is the project churning over Business Analysts which means more work for them by way of more requirements scoping meetings.

Some projects are so troubled that a Business Analyst moves on without doing any knowledge transfer which means the incoming Business Analyst has to start from scratch. In these less-than-ideal circumstances, the Business Analyst transitioning to this project can do the following.

Review Existing Documentation

The first stop on any project assignment is to review the documentation on the company SharePoint and intranet web sites for any project-related documentation. The documentation on these sites will inform the Business Analyst about the sort of trouble they may be in where requirements are concerned. These web sites are also the repositories for a lot of information related to the project, for example, the business decisions that led to the conception of the project, the pain points the company is facing, and the overall strategic direction of the business or organization. This action allows a Business Analyst to evaluate what they have and how they will plug existing information gaps.

Interface with Project Actors

Interfacing with ex-project team members or current project team members starting with the Project Manager, Project Sponsor, Product Manager, and other project team members elicits useful information for the Business Analyst trying to find their feet. This is very useful as a Business Analyst plots a course of action on a new project. Didn't I mention that this action builds a rapport with project members? It does, and it's important because these team members are going to be the Business Analyst's support crew for the life span of the project.

Rapport with End Users and Stakeholders

Taking a 5-minute call to touch base with end users and stakeholders, introducing oneself and briefly stating that this is a fact-finding call is sure to open the minds of even the most intransigent end users and stakeholders.

With this introduction, the Business Analyst can then inquire about previous requirements and where they can be found. This informal meeting is about building a rapport and getting started on a clean slate with end users and stakeholders. If the information the Business Analyst is seeking has been already been compiled, then they usually provide it or advise where it can be found, and if it doesn't exist, then the Business Analyst will start the elicitation process.

The other scenario where its already been provided and the Business Analyst cannot find it is a little tricky for the Business Analyst has to tactfully prepare the ground for restarting the elicitation process all over.

Leverage Multiple Information Sources

While it is tempting for a Business Analyst to think that their project challenges are unique, the reality is that another project or organization somewhere else has experienced the same challenges (if not worse) and lived to document it somewhere on Google.

The point being that in this day and age of massive technological changes with countless organizations undertaking the same digital transformation projects, it is very unlikely that a challenge will be unique to a particular project. A Business Analyst getting sleepless nights from never-ending project challenges is spoilt for choice if they are truly interested in finding an organization or project that has successfully triaged a similar problem before.

There are the Subject Matter Experts who are also end users or stakeholders and project team members on the internal side who can offer all manner of assistance and insights to a Business Analyst lost at sea. Then there are deeply experienced Business Analyst practitioners, influencers, thought leaders, bloggers, online publications, community groups, meet ups, social media groups, and organizations like the International Institute of Business Analysis (IIBA). These individuals, entities, and groups are external to the project, but Business Analysts can connect with them to leverage their know-how, deep expertise, and connections to resolve seemingly intractable problems. Business Analysts should not have to carry these burdens by themselves: they have been carried before by others, and Business Analysts ought to leverage that know-how for themselves and their projects.

The basic objective of not reinventing the wheel is to save the Business Analyst lots of rework and time; prevent burnout, and most importantly avoid afflicting end users and stakeholders with requirements fatigue.

While reinventing the wheel sounds like a pointer for Business Analysts joining projects that are already in motion, some of these concepts can be applied to new or greenfield projects as well.

There Is No Need to Know Everything

It may be tempting for a newly reassigned Business Analyst to try and literally become an overnight expert on the processes he/she will be focusing on changing during the requirements scoping process. This is usually because there is so much information that the Business Analyst needs to compile and make sense of as they scope requirements and simultaneously defend those requirements before project team members. For organizations that are well-structured and organized, that information will be a deluge that can literally swamp and overwhelm the Business Analyst.

In my experience, there are two caveats to this headless chicken approach.

The first one is that a lot of this information is not relevant to the pain points faced by end users and which form the backbone of the requirements that will be scoped by Business Analysts. Reviewing process documentation that is unrelated to the problems faced by end users is a waste of time; this time is better spent analyzing the actual processes and products end users want to change.

The second caveat is that Business Analysts don't have to know everything; in fact, they are better served by showing up to requirements meetings, actively listening, and asking probing questions. During this time Business Analysts should make the most of the "fresh pair of eyes" perspective because they are seeing and hearing the project concepts for the first time. This first-time effect puts them in a great position to view what is going on with new thinking and perspectives.

In my initial Business Analyst years, I stressed out over taking in as much information in as short a time as possible. This was until I noticed that the senior Business Analysts were the calmest folks in the room despite the fact that they knew just as little (if not less) about the requirements than I did. In fact, they were unflustered by the fact that they didn't know everything. How were they getting by without the sort of in-depth knowledge I was stressing out about? And therein lies the essence of this hack; Business Analysts don't need to know *everything* about a system, process, or application to scope requirements or support the project delivery process.

Here's a few ways this hack can work for Business Analysts.

Leverage Subject Matter Experts

The reality is that end users and stakeholders will always be far more knowledgeable than Business Analysts about the processes and products that need to be transformed. That's their job, and there is a name for these sorts of resources: Subject Matter Experts. It's why most projects have them, and even where none is designated, a Business Analyst can find one who can help them get under the hood of a process, system, or application. Business Analysts need to leverage these brains to drastically shorten learning curves.

Use of Humility and Vulnerability

Asking for help from end users shows humility and vulnerability on the part of Business Analysts, and it usually elicits useful insights that plug information gaps. I have been on many projects where end users allowed me to shadow them—as a supervisor would—so that I could get a feel of what the pain points in their processes were. Viewing their problems firsthand was far more insightful than any requirements workshop I could have convened to discuss their pain points.

Suppressing Impostor Syndrome

Business Analysts will occasionally be gripped by impostor syndrome where they feel their knowledge of end user requirements is inadequate and they could be exposed anytime as a fraud or fake. This translates into overblown fears that Business Analysts have about not being able to authoritatively issue responses about different scenarios and uses cases pertaining to end user requirements. This fear is real, and I still experience it sometimes on new assignments; I live in fear of being uncovered as a charade where some requirements are concerned. It was difficult overcoming impostor syndrome until a Business Analyst I worked with pointed out that she banished it when she discovered she didn't need to know everything.

This hack is not to posit that Business Analysts do not need to equip themselves with functional knowledge about the processes they are changing. While they need that functional knowledge, they can get by with actively listening and eliciting the information they need from end users and stakeholders. This approach also has the added benefit of building relationships and improving project team collaboration.

Understanding the Limitations of Technology

The vast majority of enterprise technology products have limitations, and there are some components requested by end users and stakeholders that cannot be delivered at that moment. This is the same for most of the software products we use in our lives, from mobile applications that freeze without explanation to applications that slow down with increased traffic.

That said, there will always be a workaround that can remediate the limitation. The caveat is that the workaround usually costs more to deliver given the customizations needed to remediate the limitation and remove it.

Business Analysts who understand the technology they are working with and its limitations are in a better position to set end user and stakeholder expectations as well as wring better concessions from them during negotiations.

While technology can bring efficiencies to organizations, it's important for Business Analysts to be cognizant of what technology can do and what it cannot do. It is not the foolproof silver bullet most organizations are seeking that will eternally banish their problems.

I took a while coming around to this concept, but swimming at the deep end of the Business Analyst practice quickly clarified it for me. That clarification made stakeholder negotiations and explanations easier to navigate.

Managing Fear

Projects will sometimes be so chaotic; it feels like the project is falling apart at the seams as there are problems and challenges of all types and magnitudes. How does a Business Analyst stay on top of the chaos? By staying calm, courageous, and avoiding panic. This does not mean Business Analysts shouldn't be afraid, it just means that they have control over their fears, both founded and unfounded.

It's OK to be afraid, specifically being afraid of failure, being flamed, being the fall guy, and the ultimate, getting axed. Those are all painful and negative things we wouldn't wish on our worst enemies, but they should not be the reason Business Analysts come to work every morning

Mastering fear equips a Business Analyst with a crystal-clear mind freed from worries like the fear of failure or blame while focusing solely on delivering their immediate deliverables which are the requirements they scoped yesterday. Mastery of fear exudes calmness, confidence, rational thought, and intelligent analyses when the project seems to be going up in smoke.

Business Analysts who have been in the practice for a while have hacks they swear by and have tales to tell about how those hacks have bolted them from the trickiest of spots. What about you? Do you have a hack you swear by? It must be pointed out that the best hacks are legal and do not cause a Business Analyst to compromise their integrity. Additionally, they can be passed onto other Business Analysts who may be struggling with a similar problem or situation. The wider point though is that they work, they are efficient, and they save Business Analysts a lot of time during the execution of their assignments.

When It's Time to Move On

Software development projects are staffed by people like and you me, and where human beings are involved, things can sometimes get out of hand. There will be incessant conflicts on projects, and there will be expectations that are unrealistic, impossible, and downright unprofessional.

It is understandable that the business landscape of the day can put an organization and its projects in complex and highly challenging situations. Managing these situations is not for everyone, and it requires deep expertise and specialized skillsets that can be deployed to enable a project successfully emerge from these trying situations.

When faced with complex and unpredictable project situations, some end users, stakeholders, and project actors rise to the occasion and successfully close out hair-raising situations without rancor, personal conflicts, or unprofessionalism. These challenges bring out the best in them.

Conversely the unpredictable situations on projects can bring out the worst in some end users, stakeholders, and project actors. Because they are not adequately equipped with the experience or the tools necessary to manage the unexpected challenges that arise on projects, their responses are precisely those that exacerbate and inflame project challenges. Their responses range from management by bullying or intimidation, making unrealistic demands, shirking key decisions, managing through cliques, and all manner of unprofessional operational methods.

© Roni Lubwama 2020
R. Lubwama, *The Inside Track to Excelling As a Business Analyst*,
https://doi.org/10.1007/978-1-4842-5543-8_10

Any Business Analyst who has been a practitioner for a while has likely come across both sets of projects—those that rise to the occasion when the heat is on and those that wilt under pressure. As expected, no Business Analyst looks forward to being part of the dumpster fire that is the latter option, and the rest of the chapter will detail how to spot these troubled projects.

These dumpster fires of projects induce stress and confusion amidst a lack of clarity of purpose or focus. The way these projects are run also upsets the collaborative ethic on projects, damages relationships, creates unnecessary conflicts, and in some cases makes project actors physically ill. In an ideal world, none of us would want to shorten our lives by being staffed on these types of badly run projects. Sadly, there will be points in the career of a Business Analyst when they find themselves in the midst of such projects.

Additionally, given the aforementioned downsides of being staffed on such a project, the time comes when a Business Analyst has to evaluate whether continuing their tenure on such a project is worth it.

A project that is run with no sign of operational improvements or any strategic course correction from project leadership is usually a sign for the Business Analyst to reconsider their tenure on the project. It is time to either find another project or organization or both.

Should Business Analysts just skip town the moment they hit troubled waters? Not at all.

If a Business Analyst is confident and they have the tools, the expertise, and the support of project leadership to pull the project out of the fire then by all means they ought to proceed. Keep in mind that a rescued project makes for good reading on a well-crafted resume or LinkedIn profile; it's great for career bragging rights. Not only does saving the project sharpen the intellect of a Business Analyst; it also deepens their expertise. They can always look back on how they rescued a seemingly lost cause and apply the same skillsets and expertise to other struggling projects.

However, there are projects that not even superheroes can salvage—they are that far down the rabbit hole. The project leadership lacks direction or know-how, and the project has flubbed and continues to flub key project management indices like budget, scope, and timing. Short of a change in the project or organizational leadership, there is not much that a superhero Business Analyst can do to salvage such projects. For a Business Analyst staffed on this horror show, it is time to move on.

I usually hear refrains like it's too soon to move on or it looks bad on a resume if a Business Analyst has many positions within a few months of each other. These perspectives are acceptable as long as these counter-perspectives are also given serious consideration:

- Projects with bad leadership are a career accident waiting to happen which is usually manifested by projects being mothballed, downgraded, or outright terminated. A Business Analyst could very easily be rendered jobless when a project is shuttered. Its best for Business Analysts to exit on their terms and be fully in control of the narrative about their exit.

- Badly run projects stunt professional growth not just for Business Analysts but for other team members too. If the project actors are obsessed with corporate politics and meritocracy is a dirty word, the fine work or potential of a Business Analyst is very unlikely to shine in such an environment. It's pointless for a Business Analyst to invest their future in a project obsessed with office politics.

Here are a few signs that your project and specifically your tenure as a Business Analyst on that project needs serious re-evaluation.

Unrealistic Expectations or Assignments

While Business Analysts will wear many hats during the life of a project, some of the hats they are asked to wear are straight out of crazy town. I know; I have been asked to wear one such hat.

I had been on a project for a few months when I was asked when I was going to remove "X" from the project. Stunning but true: I was being asked to "fire" one of the project team members. There was so much wrong with this jaw-dropping request that I didn't know where to start or end.

This has been touched on in the beginning chapters of this book: Business Analysts are rarely given the authority to hire or fire other project team members. They may interview or advise which candidate to hire or which disruptive team member needs to have a "chat" with human resources, but that's the limit of their hiring or firing powers.

There may be projects out there where the project structure gives a Business Analyst these kinds of powers, but I will hazard a guess that they are a very tiny minority.

This particular instance was so galling for the simple reason that the Project Manager was simply avoiding their project staffing responsibilities. There had been no discussion about why such a sensitive task was being delegated to me, and it just smacked of high-handed unprofessionalism.

This episode illustrates the meaning of unrealistic expectations or assignments that Business Analysts encounter on projects.

Another take on unrealistic expectation's centers on impossible workloads that regardless of how hard and long a Business Analyst works, the workload cannot be brought under control. A good day is a 12-hour shift for a Business Analyst on a project of this type. Unrelenting workloads are usually a sign that something is off-kilter in terms of project objectives, stakeholder expectations, project staffing, or the style of working of an individual Business Analyst.

Long shifts are unhealthy; they can induce burnout, not to mention that they are unhelpful toward maintaining a healthy work life balance. Experiencing these downsides of difficult workloads for extended periods of time should cause a Business Analyst to reevaluate if this is the ideal Business Analyst career they had in mind.

Another sign a project may not be right for Business Analyst is when project management works at cross-purposes and sees nothing wrong with that way of working.

If these expectations or assignments are being set with regularity with the expectation that the Business Analyst will meet, them then it may be time to consider if the Business Analyst is on the right project. More importantly they have to evaluate if this is how they would like to grow their career and professional abilities.

Lack of Transparency or Integrity

Project management that is lacking in transparency or integrity will sooner or later get a Business Analyst burned professionally. Project leadership that is brazenly deceptive and which prizes the same behaviors from other project team members should cause a Business Analyst to evaluate their tenure on such a project.

I once witnessed a project manager outrightly deceive organizational leadership about the status of the project I was staffed on. For starters he fibbed that the project was green—only that it wasn't. It was trending red and had major issues with funding given the challenges it was having with closing out major project milestones.

On that call I was hearing a description of a project far removed from the one I was staffed on. All the warts were conveniently sanitized, and the impression the other callers got was that the project was going well; nothing could have been further from the truth.

This deception was unnecessary and it deflated my morale as it was obvious I was not on board with these brazen deceptions. This brazen act of dishonesty told me everything I needed to know about him, his values, and more importantly where our project was headed under his stewardship.

The person who lies to your face is not interested in your success or that of the project that he manages; it's just their interests they are looking out for. This lack of integrity was a sign it was time to consider other options.

Purposefully Poor Communication

A close relative of a lack of integrity. If a Business Analyst is finding out about critical decisions concerning their work through the grapevine or informal unverified channels, then there is a problem. When project leadership is not getting ahead of major decisions and leaving them to be communicated by the grapevine, then what you have is not a communication problem but a zero-communication problem.

I once found out that end users and stakeholders had pulled the plug on the requirements we had been scoping and were instead moving in a totally different direction. Project management knew about this 360-degree turn, but we the Business Analysts were in the dark and continued working those same requirements. The point here is that information that impacts a Business Analyst at the tactical level has to be available to them, and they don't need to beg to access it.

If this is a one-off event, that is understandable, but if this is how project management operates, the Business Analyst is courting trouble, for they will be working at cross-purposes most of the time. To my mind there are fewer surefire ways to make a Business Analyst look incompetent than denying them information that is critical to their deliverables.

Ingrained Lack of Focus and Purpose

It is the nature of organizational management that not all organizations and project setups are efficient and supremely organized to deliver all the objectives they set out to deliver. Organizations and project setups are also different; some of them are great at project execution and others not so much. Additionally, organizations always seek maximum returns from the projects they undertake; in other words, they will undertake those projects with the biggest bang for their buck.

In realizing this objective, some organizations have mastered the dynamics of successfully delivering multiple high-impact projects simultaneously. Other organizations cannot even come close as attempts to run multiple projects end in dismal failures or very few of the original project objectives are achieved as they undertake these multiple fronts and high-impact project implementation approach.

In terms of project performance, you can always tell the high achievers from the slackers after spending a few weeks with an organization.

There will be projects that sound and look dated—they just don't close. Others close as soon as they are launched while others are in perpetual state of "launching."

Watercooler chitchat can be amusing if not frightening as that is how I once found out the project I had been assigned to never gets anything done but for one thing: chewing up and throwing out team members. It had been in motion for so long colleagues started called it the "zombie" project.

While staying on zombie projects likely guarantees job security, it is not the type of project you want to be on forever. The reason it most likely never closes is due to lack of focus, purpose, and direction or all three.

Additionally, if a Business Analyst keeps getting assigned to projects that fold almost as soon as they are launched, those talents and abilities are being mismanaged, and it's time to consider other professional pursuits. Launching a project is expensive business so why close projects willy nilly? What would be the thinking behind such project launches in the first place? It is the type of thinking and actions that display a lack of focus and clarity at the organizational and project level that don't bode for a Business Analyst career.

Toxic Organizational Cultures

There is a ton of stuff that's considered toxic on projects that cannot be exhaustively covered here, but suffice to say that if a project environment repeatedly makes a Business Analyst intimidated, physically unsafe, stressed out, or ostracized, then it's time for a tenure re-evaluation.

Under the guise of competitive creativity, some projects encourage pitting team members against each other. I am all for healthy competition that gets the creative juices flowing, but an environment where the worst office politics is conflated with competitive creativity is best avoided altogether. Very rarely do project teams produce outstanding deliverables in such toxic environments. It's also unlikely that a gifted and talented Business Analyst will stand out as meritocracy is not exactly valued in such project environments.

Closely following toxic cultures is cronyism or "buddyism." It simply refers to project environments that closely mimic *Animal Farm* where the Napoleons reign supreme and where there are few if any consequences when they don't meet their deliverables. On these, projects' accountability and responsibility for project deliverables are applied selectively, and some project team members become notorious for being perennially late on their deliverables. Because they are buddies of project management, they do not face any sanctions, or if they do face sanctions, it's more of a charade.

In fact, sanctions are so selectively and lackadaisically applied by project management that team members may be sanctioned based on how project managers feel on any given morning. Cronyism does not bode well for project teams whose lifeblood is collaboration, accountability, unity of purpose and cohesiveness, and this is usually manifested in the quality of the deliverables put out by the project team.

There are many more challenging project environments out there, and I am certain more experienced Business Analysts than me have more colorful tales that they could tell about projects and project management that have lost their marbles.

These tales are just a microcosm of how off-balance some projects can be. The moral of these tales is to get Business Analysts to do regular spot-checks and review whether the project environment is meeting the objectives that a Business Analyst envisioned when they were hired. This is especially the case if project management isn't interested in rectifying these maladies in which event a Business Analyst urgently needs that career re-evaluation.

Afterword

Remember how this book opened? This was my exclamation:

"This job sucks"!

Does it suck anymore? Certainly not, and it has turned out to be an intellectually and professionally rewarding career. Truth is at that time and in that moment, I lacked the tools and skillsets that could have taken the "sucking" out of my Business Analyst roles.

My Business Analyst career in those formative years was more valleys than crests, and to say it was difficult would be putting it mildly. There were so many times when giving up and trying my talents elsewhere seemed not only the obvious choice but the logical one as well.

To demonstrate how difficult it was, I held three Business Analyst positions in under 2 years—an average of 8 months per position! While the reasons for those exits were varied, at its core it came down to the fact that I wasn't ready for Business Analyst prime time. While I was technically competent, I lacked many of the non-technical skills illustrated in this book which would have enhanced my effectiveness from the get-go.

This steep learning curve was flattened through a combination of self-study, observation, tutoring, and practice.

© Roni Lubwama 2020
R. Lubwama, *The Inside Track to Excelling As a Business Analyst*,
https://doi.org/10.1007/978-1-4842-5543-8_11

On this journey I have seen Business Analysts struggling in exactly the same ways I struggled. I have also encountered potential Business analysts seeking the secret handshakes[1] that will make them great Business Analysts. It does not have to be this way.

The purpose of this book is to demonstrate that anyone who equips them-selves with these non-technical skills will excel as a Business Analyst. In the process it dispels the notion that secret handshakes are required in the mak-ing of outstanding Business Analysts.

Since you have come this far, I hope that you have found these principles for Business Analyst excellence applicable and of use to whatever career you are pursuing at the moment. Yes, that's right; these principles are not restricted to information technology (IT) Business Analysts; anyone can apply them to their career situation.

Can the book be improved? Definitely, and I look forward to hearing from you. Feel free to send me those nuggets of wisdom via LinkedIn direct mes-saging: https://www.linkedin.com/in/roni-lubwama-b2a65518/.

Here is wishing you a very successful Business Analyst career!

---

[1] A handshake used by an exclusive society to secretly identify and acknowledge each other.

Bonus Skill: Managing Wafflers

This appendix considers one of the most difficult challenges that Business Analysts will encounter during the process of delivering software development projects. It is those moments when project actors, more specifically end users and stakeholders, cannot make up their minds as to what to expect from a software product whose development a Business Analyst has been assigned to oversee. Let's consider the waffle in a little more detail.

One of the most insidious aspects of the Business Analyst line of work is encountering what I refer to as the waffle or waffling. In the world of business, it is known as indecision.

Simply put, to waffle is to "fail to make up one's mind." To flip-flop, vacillate, and equivocate are fancier ways of saying you are waffling. While I have heard waffling also referred to as "stalling," the two are different though related activities.

Going forward I will refer to those who waffle as wafflers. The idea is not to apply the word "wafflers" as a derogatory term but to illustrate the dynamics of the waffle. For our purposes, the waffling referred to here is the type indulged in by end users, stakeholders, and a host of other project actors.

© Roni Lubwama 2020
R. Lubwama, *The Inside Track to Excelling As a Business Analyst*,
https://doi.org/10.1007/978-1-4842-5543-8

Waffling or indecision is one of those aspects of the Business Analyst practice that stymies even the most battle-hardened Business Analysts mainly because of the haphazard way it manifests. Your assignment may be on schedule, but for some reason, critical decisions don't come in time or they come late, or you need to wrangle them out of people. There are information gaps or decision gaps, and you are unsure whether you are dealing with just minor operational gaps or black holes. In extreme cases the critical decisions do not come at all, eventually leading to the assignment or project being pulled.

This is what makes waffling so dangerous to assignments or projects. As a modus operandi, waffling is largely impervious to technical skills or jargon and to effectively nullify the waffle, a Business Analyst requires more people smarts than technical gifts.

Essentially the waffler makes a decision one moment and then just as quickly reverses it the next. Like a pendulum the waffler will swing between different positions at any given time. Granted *some* sort of decisions are being made, but they are constantly in flux. It's apt to refer to them as *pseudo*-decisions. They are decisions when the waffler wants them to be decisions. They eventually become decisions when the issue is forced by an external factor like a looming hard stop or nonnegotiable deadline.

Having encountered wafflers on multiple software development projects, I can now tell inside a few meetings that I have a waffler "situation" on my hands. Obviously, being a waffler is not a capital offense, but waffling on a time-boxed project or assignment ought to be legislated as a crime of sorts. This is because a resource who cannot make up their mind is stealing your time and everyone else's time, not to mention the project's time. There is also a more critical reason why you should be concerned with the waffler's antics that are freezing your progress: they are stalling the project delivery process.

But first, the anatomy of a typical waffle.

User A determines that they need changes made to an application, process, or system. You, the Business Analyst, and User A agree on the changes—which is referred to as the scope of work. You and another actor we shall refer to as Actor A deliver the changes initially requested by User A. This is usually done by showing User A the prototype that represents the changes that have been made. User A partially approves the prototype and requests you to make more changes to some aspects of the prototype.

Just to be clear, I am not against such changes, and a few changes here and there are acceptable; that is the point of using iterative software development methodologies like Agile. Urgent changes can be made to software, processes, or systems in real time to reflect current marketplace conditions. To repeat, it's perfectly acceptable for end users like User A to request urgent changes to prototypes before they are launched.

But what happens if User A is in the habit of requesting changes every time you demonstrate the prototype? I have been on software development projects where User A types literally request changes *every time* you engage them. What they requested last week is unimportant, and they have a new fad today that they would like you to work on right now. They have a bucket list of never-ending change requests that they spring on you every time you present the previous phase's work.

Shockingly sometimes the requested changes are the changes that were initially made, initially rejected, and are now back in vogue again. This is the essence of the waffler and the act of waffling. Countless times, with frustration getting the better of me, I have wanted to tell stakeholders, "please make up your mind!" The changes range from the subtle to the minor to the major, but ultimately, they still hold up progress and impede closure of the project or assignment. Not to mention how adversely these antics impact project financials and timelines with none other than you having to answer for the unsightly mess that the project will soon become.

The tinkering waffler is merely one type. Another type of waffler is a stakeholder who will not commit to *any* one decision. They are always consulting, or they are "busy." When you do get a decision, there is a caveat: the team or their manager may change that same decision anytime. This is an especially painful type of waffling for Business Analysts because they rely on this input from stakeholders to do their work. Without this input, they might as well stay home. I clearly recall the times when I was "waiting for a decision" for the umpteenth time, and I have never felt as inept as I did in those moments.

Did I mention project financials and timelines? Wafflers act like these things are for lesser mortals to worry about. Wafflers inhabit a parallel universe where the impacts arising from unlimited change requests do not concern them.

This may sound like fiction, but wafflers are real, and they are out there wrecking projects even as I write this. In times of raging angst brought on by wafflers, I always wondered why anyone or wafflers for that matter would work this way. It stresses out everyone involved with the project, and in the very short term, nobody looks forward to working with the waffler. The waffler's credibility and reputation—if they have one—take a serious beating.

Reasons for Waffling

Different wafflers have different reasons for waffling, but there are some general reasons why people choose to waffle should the opportunity present itself. In no particular order, these are some reasons that give rise to waffling.

Minimal Domain Knowledge

In lay terms, it is the knowledge or expertise you possess about a given subject or field. Your expertise about a subject does not have to be advanced, but you should possess enough expertise to logically explain the need and the potential impacts if your request goes unfulfilled.

To my mind this is one of the main drivers of waffling. The waffler does not have adequate knowledge of what they seek to change. Due to knowledge gaps (which the waffler dares not to admit to), anybody working with a waffler will be stuck in an endless loop of back and forth. A painful guessing game whose objective is to figure out an end point or destination. In reality, the waffle is merely a smokescreen for existing knowledge gaps on the waffler's part.

If the waffler worked smarter, this would be a non-issue. I have seen other folks who had the same knowledge gaps but simply brought along a more knowledgeable sidekick to do the heavy lifting.

Managerial Vacuums

In an ideal world, our managers would want to know why we are still chasing the same assignment three months after we committed to close it.

More importantly they would want to know what we are doing to correct this messy state of affairs. That's why they are managers, and that's what they are paid to do. This ideal world does not apply to the waffler as they can chase the same assignment—making a tweak here and there—with no serious repercussions from their manager. From the outside it appears the waffler has minimal managerial direction, guidance, leadership, or all three.

It need not be mentioned that in the absence of managerial guidance, this vacuum will be quickly supplanted by the waffler and his/her waffling ways. And while we are not always privy to managerial supervision of subordinates, the presence of waffling and the chasing of regurgitated, fluffy, never-ending assignments are usually signs of ineffective managerial oversight.

Managerial Incoherence

Does your manager inspire such confidence in you that you go over and above to get stuff done for them? Ditto the process and systems you work with. Conversely, does your manager induce murderous thoughts just by thinking about them? I know that feeling. I have been there in a previous life.

A manager or process or system that is stultifying, that is an absolute kill joy; who wants to stake a reputation on them? Think of the last time your manager asked you to do something at 9:09am and changed it at 9:22am without any reason or they provided a fudgy reason at best (of the dog ate my homework type).

What if those types of changes were being made every week or with such regularity that you were left dazed by the changes? How would you respond the next time your manager or whoever makes these changes asked you to defend them before a review board? There is no certainty that the position you just defended will still be in place by the time you made your closing pitch. I know how I would feel. I would want to do *nothing*.

I would vacillate between different positions until I knew where my manager stood. That is of course until his/her next flip-flop. If the decision came down to either saving my abused reputation or saving project financials, I think you know who would get thrown under the bus. Project financials be damned.

A waffler in this situation is in a catch-22 situation. They are in an unwinnable situation and just trying to do the best that will save their hide. This is one of those instances where I fully root for the waffler.

Buying Time

Sometimes the waffle exists because the waffler is buying time. They under-stand they have a knowledge gap, so they jam the wheels of progress as they get a handle on the material they ought to be articulating to other project actors like Business Analysts.

Is it an expensive way to learn anything? You bet. But it works for the waffler. While I understand this type of waffler, for at least there is an admission that they have knowledge gaps that need to be closed, I find waffling as a remedy distasteful.

Motivations for Change

Wafflers in this situation come in two flavors. The first type loathes and dis-trusts the process and systems so intensely that they will do *anything* to change them or eradicate them. Anything. If that means making multiple requests in 30 days, so be it. They couldn't care less who dies in the process much less care for project financials.

In reality this type of constant tinkering and tweaking if focused will likely produce positive outcomes. It's just that it's a massive headache if you are on the receiving end of all those never-ending change requests. The second type stopped caring last year and does not really care what happens to the assign-ment. They change things on a whim confident that they will not have to handle the future fallout from their shabby decisions today.

How Business Analysts Can Manage Wafflers

But how do you inoculate yourself against wafflers and their mayhem? It depends on your situation, but there are a few surefire ways to manage wafflers. These items have worked wonders for me in the past, and you may want to give them a test drive.

Create and Use Guardrails

Guardrails on roads and car seatbelts are put in place to save us from ourselves, like when we drive above the speed limit while simultaneously texting and having breakfast.

In the same vein, you need guardrails to keep you away from the worst impulses of wafflers and their handlers. Here's what guardrails would look like:

1. An iterative software development methodology like Agile can mitigate this mayhem if you stick to it the way it was designed. Essentially the waffler cannot change the scope of work at will.

   There has to be a time and process to review and process new work requests. Lock down this process and follow it to the letter. Even better, let the wafflers know that this is how it will work. If they stray, beat them into line (not literally).

2. Tolerate the waffler once and they will be back for more. Just like schoolyard bullies. Let it be known that while you are willing to be flexible, there will be limits. And that flexibility has to bend to the law of the land—see point 1 above. This mitigation strategy is largely down to you and what principles you are willing to espouse and defend.

3. Don't play this game solo. Anytime you are up against a waffler, expect progress challenges of some sort at some point. Mitigate this by drawing in other stakeholders to this slow-motion train wreck. The stakeholders do not have to do the chasing for you; you are only making them aware of the likely consequences based on the current trajectory. For example, critical deadlines will be missed if this waffling continues unchecked.

Motivations for Waffling

When you understand where the waffler is coming from and more importantly why they are waffling, then there is no need to pull out clumps of your hair. Take the time to understand what type of waffler you are dealing with.

This knowledge is critical in devising remedies for the waffler. For instance, if it is knowledge gaps and assuming you know which knowledge gaps they have, you can tactfully fill in those gaps. Is that how they run their shop? Then it's time to inform both the shop attendant and manager that their actions (or lack of) are sure to end in failure if they don't change their ways.

Bonus Interpersonal Skill: Credibility and Reputation

Credibility comes down to whether you can be trusted or whether you are believable. Your reputation is the perception other people have of you. You earn a reputation by the actions you take or don't take.

As a Business Analyst, do you meet your deadlines? When you commit to an action, do you act on it and see it through to its conclusion? More importantly, is there an understanding that you are a major piece in the puzzle? A piece so important that the puzzle is almost useless without it? How you consistently respond to these situations is what builds your reputation and makes you credible.

When you are trusted, then people, systems, and processes come to rely on you to get things done. The more you accomplish, the more responsibilities you get, and eventually your career ambitions—whatever they may be—start

© Roni Lubwama 2020
R. Lubwama, *The Inside Track to Excelling As a Business Analyst*,
https://doi.org/10.1007/978-1-4842-5543-8

to snowball upwards. It's a vicious cycle of old-fashioned goodness compounding itself. Conversely, when you are unreliable, people, systems, and processes do not fully trust you. They may trust you with serious stuff but only grudgingly or because they have no options.

When you say, "no worries, consider it done," that's a cue for bouts of nail-biting tension as a positive outcome is not guaranteed. Your "no worries, consider it done" sounds eerily like "be very worried, and consider it undone." Again, it's a vicious cycle that compounds itself leaving you with a radioactive aura that is difficult though not impossible to shake off.

In sum your past results define your present reality. There is a reason why the English language has the expression, his/her reputation precedes him/her. In lay terms, you are known by what you have done in the past: good or bad. Unfortunately, a bad reputation and a lack of credibility cannot be easily laundered by flaunting deep technical expertise.

For a Business Analyst, technical expertise counts for very little if you have next to zero credibility. On the contrary, I have seen it work like a charm in reverse; a Business Analyst with minimal technical expertise builds a stellar reputation merely by delivering on their commitments flawlessly. It certainly helps knowing your way around technically, but if you are in the market for an enhanced reputation, executing better is your best bet.

But how do reputations become tarnished when we are hired and assigned to projects on the understanding that we are credible and that we can be trusted to deliver?

How Business Analysts Tarnish Their Credibility and Reputations

Many ways come to mind as to how a whistle-clean reputation can be sullied in record time. Some people have reputations as complainers or are excessive gossips or are just lacking in basic professional etiquette. While these are not appealing traits, they are not really reputation killers and we eventually learn to manage the people who have them. However, there is a category of traits and behaviors that Business Analysts should avoid as they are the ulti-mate reputation killers. These reputation shredders are so routine that they do not seem out of place in corporate settings. The fact that they are so common-place does not mean that they cannot harm your reputation. Nothing could be further from the truth as I consider the most egregious ones.

Overpromising and Underdelivering

Occasionally, we will overpromise stuff when we want to catch the eye of our manager or some other C-suite type; we want them to know how hardworking and smart we are. We will take on more projects than we can handle or commit to impossible timelines. You have to know your limits to play this game effectively. Some people play this game and ace it all the time. Get it wrong repeatedly, and it's a guaranteed way to single-handedly trash your reputation.

Avoid this game like the plague unless you have what it takes to close multiple assignments at the same time. Better to catch the eye of the manager by executing well on a few assignments than bombing out on the many.

Deception

We cannot avoid the occasional silly little lies or the innocuous tall tales. But deception or consistently misstating stuff will in short order brand you as someone lacking in credibility or trust or both. It's also critical to know when to fib and on which subject to fib for the consequences have never been more different.

Inflating the square footage of your mansion at a social outing is largely harmless, but a habit of blithely spouting falsehoods on projects is a surefire way to torch your credibility. Consider this the cyanide of reputations—it will seriously jeopardize your credibility. It always puzzles me why anybody thinks deception is a cool way of working in the 21st century.

Sloppiness

If you consistently go about your assignments without demanding high standards of yourself, don't be surprised when your work comes across as sloppy. And with sloppiness comes a tarnished reputation. It's not enough to merely cross the finishing line; it counts much more when the finished product is beyond reproach.

I have been sent meeting invites only for the folks who convene the meetings to ghost[1] me and the other attendees. Even worse are the folks who volunteer to work on an assignment and half the time they have no idea what is going on with the assignment they "volunteered" to close out. Then there are the proposals I have seen sent to senior management strewn with very basic grammatical errors.

---

[1] When someone cuts off all communication with another person without reason or warning.

Unbelievable as it sounds, grammatical errors still happen in this day and age where word processors are powered by artificial intelligence. This is very simple stuff: you convene meetings; attend them. You volunteer for something; get it done. Sneering that you are too busy to mind misplaced commas or apostrophes? Then consider the fact that a manager reviewing such an error-strewn proposal would have doubts entrusting you with major responsibilities if you cannot be bothered cleaning up trivial stuff like grammar. This is one of the easiest reputation shredders to get rid of, but surprise, surprise, it's very much alive in many professional settings. Only Bill Gates[2] and his ilk get a pass on this one.

Slacking

A close relative of sloppiness. Let's assume you have regularly scheduled status meetings or progress checkpoints that assess whether you are on track to meet your objectives. Ever notice the folks who always have the *same* status update for 2 weeks straight? I am not referring to those whose progress has been genuinely hampered by the glacial pace of organizational bureaucracy.

I am referring to those folks who have no compelling reason today as to why they have not delivered what they promised to complete last week. Actually, that's not entirely true; they always have an excuse; it's the "I was busy" excuse. Another easy to eradicate reputation shredder if one applied their time efficiently. Truth be told, all one needs to do is get stuff done. Not tomorrow or next week but today.

Factual Inaccuracies

Closely related to deception. We don't always have the answers when we are asked questions. Better to play it safe with an "I don't know" or "I will check and get you an answer shortly" than proceed with a half-baked response. Do this more than is necessary, and the explanations you offer will be taken with a healthy pinch of salt.

Organizations and projects tend to lionize "quick" thinkers or those who can "think on their feet" which is admirable if you "think on your feet" with facts instead of half-truths or outright deceptions. Reminds me of a time on a call with business stakeholders when I mentioned that Leo told me that's how the

---

[2] Tom Popomaronis, "In 1994, Bill Gates replied to a stranger's email within 18 minutes—and their exchange reveals a hilarious truth about the billionaire," CNBC Make It, February 22, 2019, www.cnbc.com/2019/02/22/bill-gates-response-to-a-strangers-email-reveals-a-hilarious-truth.html. It states that Bill Gates "thinks spell-check is a waste of time."

process worked, and everyone burst into laughter. Nothing more was said, but it was obvious Leo had been providing them with inaccurate information and they saw no need to take him seriously. To them Leo was a source of amusement if not derision.

I knew Leo as a decent hardworking Business Analyst even though he had the occasional hot flushes that led him to volunteer factually inaccurate information. It's certainly beneficial to be a reference point for facts; just be sure your responses are factually accurate, and they won't saddle you with a laughable reputation like Leo.

Waffling

Waffling has already been showcased earlier in Appendix A, and it's one of those behaviors that Business Analysts should avoid like the plague. It erodes confidence and gives the impression that you don't trust your ideas or those of your team. A Business Analyst who cannot make up their mind will have a very short shelf life in this business. Do your homework, craft a position, gain consensus, exercise flexibility and be ready to intelligently defend this position.

Over-politicking

Office politics has been reviewed in greater detail in Chapter 5. Nevertheless, Business Analysts should strive to professionally achieve results without calling on backstabbing, factionalism or using foul means. More than any of the foregoing behaviors, a reputation for over-politicking is not one anyone would want to have.

A stellar reputation and being credible are must-have accessories in the Business Analyst toolkit, accessories that must be maintained at all times. A Business Analyst is largely in the business of changing minds mostly by persuasion and negotiation. Irony is a Business Analyst lacking in credibility or harboring a base reputation trying to change the minds of project stakeholders, for example. It can be done, but the work of changing minds is infinitely much harder if you are lacking in credibility or have a poor reputation. I much prefer working *smarter* than working harder.

Further Reading

General

www.salesforce.com/products/platform/what-is-digital-transformation/

www.forbes.com/sites/quora/2019/03/04/how-is-digital-transformation-different-from-change-management/#3335f82838d5

www.cmswire.com/digital-workplace/change-management-the-key-to-successful-digital-transformations/

www.prosci.com/resources/articles/change-management-definition

www.forbes.com/sites/danielnewman/2018/09/11/top-10-digital-transformation-trends-for-2019/#7d73b1333c30

www.entrepreneur.com/article/309374

www.businessanalystprofessional.com/difference-requirement-gathering-requirement-elicitation/

www.cio.com/article/3156998/agile-project-management-a-beginners-guide.html

www.stateofagile.com/#ufh-i-423641583-12th-annual-state-of-agile-report/473508

R. Lubwama, *The Inside Track to Excelling As a Business Analyst*,
https://doi.org/10.1007/978-1-4842-5543-8

Technical Skills

www.project-skills.com/what-specific-technical-skills-do-business-analysts-need-2/

www.thebalancecareers.com/business-analyst-skill-set-2062363

www.bridging-the-gap.com/business-analyst-technical-skills/

www.softwaretestinghelp.com/business-analysis-tools/

www.isixsigma.com/new-to-six-sigma/getting-started/what-six-sigma/

www.mitratech.com/resource-hub/blog/configuration-vs-customization-whats-difference-matter/

Soft Skills

www.iiba.org/iiba-analyst-catalyst-blogs/how-to-become-the-go-to-business-analyst-by-establishing-trust/

www.getsmarter.com/blog/career-advice/top-business-analysis-trends-2019/

www.linkedin.com/pulse/hot-jobs-demand-skills-russell-fairbanks/

https://hbr.org/2015/11/two-things-to-do-after-every-meeting

https://hbr.org/2015/07/the-condensed-guide-to-running-meetings

Persuasion

https://businessanalystlearnings.com/blog/2014/3/5/7-practical-ways-to-persuade-stakeholders

www.powerhomebiz.com/managing-and-growing/alliances/art-per-suasion-business-analysts.htm

Resistance to Change

www.bridging-the-gap.com/resistant-stakeholders-change/

www.bridging-the-gap.com/not-for-feint-of-heart/

www.batimes.com/articles/six-common-problems-faced-by-a-busi-ness-analyst.html

http://projectcommunityonline.com/how-business-analysts-can-help-avoid-resistance-to-change.html

Office Politics

www.inc.com/martin-zwilling/7-steps-for-navigating-office-pol-itics-even-if-yo.html

www.mindtools.com/pages/article/newCDV_85.htm

www.forbes.com/sites/travisbradberry/2015/09/15/6-ways-to-win-at-office-politics/#20eedc2716d2

Michael Armstrong, *How to Be an Even Better Manager*, 10th ed. (Kogan Publishing, 2017)

Empathy

https://elearningindustry.com/six-leadership-soft-skills-training

General Business Analyst Skills

https://theuncommonleague.com/blog/2017824/six-soft-skills-that-set-amazing-business-analysts-above-the-rest

https://businessanalystlearnings.com/business-analyst-career/2018/10/28/how-motivated-business-analysts-can-leave-a-lasting-legacy

Flexibility/Malleability

https://medium.com/@spydergrrl/https-medium-com-spydergrrl-how-to-be-a-bad-business-analyst-86a27cf09095

Body Language

https://businessanalystlearnings.com/blog/2013/6/12/body-language-the-importance-of-non-verbal-cues

www.mindtools.com/pages/article/Body_Language.htm

https://aspetraining.com/resources/blog/important-communication-skills-for-business-analysts

Facilitation

www.modernanalyst.com/Resources/Articles/tabid/115/ID/2490/
The-Twelve-Shades-of-the-Business-Analyst-BA-Facilitator.aspx

Listening

www.modernanalyst.com/Careers/InterviewQuestions/tabid/128/
ID/1305/What-is-Active-Listening-and-how-can-it-benefit-the-
business-analyst.aspx

https://businessanalystlearnings.com/business-analyst-career/
2017/10/17/5-tenets-of-active-listening

Collaboration

www.cio.com/article/2414680/why-you-need-to-break-down-the-
wall-between-business-analyst-and-qa-teams.html

www.nutcache.com/blog/the-importance-of-collaboration-in-
the-workplace/

www.pmi.org/learning/library/project-team-performance-
expected-behaviors-6759

Communication

www.modernanalyst.com/Resources/Articles/tabid/115/ID/1994/10-
Ways-to-Hone-Your-Communication-Skills-as-a-Business-Analyst.
aspx

https://theuncommonleague.com/blog/2018226/be-an-
effective-communicator-with-these-tips

https://businessanalystlearnings.com/business-analyst-
career/2014/4/21/soft-skills-for-business-analysts-
communication

https://aspetraining.com/resources/blog/important-
communication-skills-for-business-analysts

https://smallbusiness.chron.com/dangers-weak-communication-
skills-50641.html

www.batimes.com/articles/four-communication-skill-components-
that-a-professional-should-master.html

Ego Mastery

https://theuncommonleague.com/blog/manage-smartest-person

Building Relationships

www.linkedin.com/pulse/building-strong-business-relationships-analyst-boland-mba-itil/

www.batimes.com/kupe-kupersmith/how-a-business-analyst-becomes-an-advocate.html

www.bridging-the-gap.com/stakeholder-relationships/

www.nerdery.com/insights/building-trust-through-business-analysis

Emotional Intelligence

www.inc.com/marcel-schwantes/if-you-can-honestly-say-yes-to-these-7-questions-your-emotional-intelligence-is-higher-than-you-think.html

www.mindtools.com/pages/article/newLDR_45.htm

https://medium.com/personal-growth/the-10-qualities-of-an-emotionally-intelligent-person-f595440af4fb

www.inc.com/justin-bariso/ask-yourself-these-5-questions-daily-your-emotional-intelligence-will-skyrocket.html

https://positivepsychology.com/emotional-intelligence-eq/

https://hbr.org/2018/10/working-with-people-who-arent-self-aware

Creativity and Problem-Solving

www.smartsheet.com/problem-solving-techniques

Decision Making

www.modernanalyst.com/Resources/Articles/tabid/115/ID/4962/Doctor-BA-and-Making-Decisions-as-a-Business-Analyst.aspx

https://elearningindustry.com/six-leadership-soft-skills-training

www.modernanalyst.com/Resources/Articles/tabid/115/ID/2643/
An-Overview-of-the-Analytical-Thinking-and-Problem-Solving-
Soft-Skill.aspx

Collaboration

www.thebalancecareers.com/decision-making-skills-with-
examples-2063748

Strategic Thinking and Visioning

www.linkedin.com/learning/strategic-thinking

Ambiguity

www.linkedin.com/pulse/20130829124922-284615-dealing-
with-ambiguity-the-new-business-imperative

www.modernanalyst.com/Resources/Articles/tabid/115/ID/2076/
Ambiguity-Uncertainty-or-Both.aspx

www.pmi.org/learning/library/ambiguity-management-new-
frontier-6285

https://letsgrowleaders.com/2014/09/17/7-ways-to-help-your-team-deal-
with-ambiguity/

www.projectinsight.net/blogs/project-management-tips/
overcome-ambiguity-to-improve-performance

Conflict Management

www.pon.harvard.edu/daily/conflict-resolution/types-conflict/

www.pon.harvard.edu/daily/conflict-resolution/
conflict-resolution-strategies/

Index

A

ABC Corp
  business processes, 18, 19
  deployment, 24
  designing, 21
  post-deployment activities, 24
  Project Charter/project plan, 19, 20
  requirements, 20
  technical teams, 22
  test phase, 22, 23

Action parties, 75

Agile/Scrum methodology, 16, 17, 129

Ambiguity
  acceptance, 126, 127
  Agile methodology, 129
  collaboration, 128
  communication, 127
  definition, 125
  documented process, 125, 126
  failure, 126
  flexibility, 128
  indecision/waffling, 127
  information gaps, 126
  poor communication, 126
  quantities, 127
  requirements, 125
  visualization, 129

Analytical and critical thinking, 129
  analyses, 133
  bias/judgement, 135
  collaboration, 135
  communication skills, 134
  expensive mistakes, 133
  hidden use cases, 132, 133
  interconnectedness/dependencies, 130
  situation, 133
  testing and validation, 131
  users and stakeholders, 132

Analytical skills, 31

Application configuration, 42, 43

B

Body language, 63
  experience, 66
  literature, 66
  nonverbal cues, 66
  practice, 66

Building relationships
  commitments, 84
  conflict resolution, 82
  importance, 81
  information loop, 83
  listening, 82
  negotiations/persuasion, 81
  positive attitudes, 84
  professionalism, 83
  stakeholders needs, 82, 83
  willingness to learn, 83
  work relations, 81

Business Analyst (BA), 137
  business processes, 13
  challenges

© Roni Lubwama 2020
R. Lubwama, *The Inside Track to Excelling As a Business Analyst*,
https://doi.org/10.1007/978-1-4842-5543-8

Business Analyst (BA) (*cont.*)
    enforcement abilities, 46
    mind-sets/attitudes, 47
    office politics, 49
    resistance to change (see Resistance
      to Change)
    scope creep, 48
    stakeholders (see Stakeholders)
  communication problem, 149
  deception, 165
  decision-making (see Decision-making)
  definition, 8
  ego, 96
    communication skills, 97
    critique, 96
    ideas/concepts/perspectives, 96
    self-awareness, 97
  emotional intelligence
    accountability, 93
    active listening, 93
    role-play, 92
    social skills, 93
  emotions, 84
  expectations/assignments, 147, 148
  focus and purpose, lack of, 149, 150
  hack (see Hack, BA)
  interpersonal skills, 112
  operational improvements, 146
  perspectives, 146
  practitioner, 146
  problems, 9, 113
    act with urgency, 115
    concert, project team, 114, 115
    data and facts, 114
  productivity and efficiency, 13
    project management
      structures, 13, 14
    SDLC, 14, 15
    tools and methodologies, 13
  reputation, 164
  requirements
    documentation, 11
    elicitation process, 10, 11
    signed-off, 11, 12
  role in future, 8
  sloppiness, 165, 166
  solution providers, 12
  toxic on projects, 150, 151
  transparency/integrity, 148, 149
  underdeliver, 165
  waffling, 167
  work, 8
  work content, 9
Business process modeling, 33
  flow diagram, 33
Business Requirement
    Document (BRD), 11

C

Change management, 2
  BA, 5
  project management, 5
  technological platforms, 2
  tectonic shifts, 2, 4
Collaboration, 104
  communication, 106
  flexible/compromise, 105
  information sharing, 105
  partiality, 105
  problem-solving capabilities, 104
  product delivery, 104
  team members, 105
Communication skills, 53, 77
  importance
    conflicts, 57
    credibility, 57
    information gaps, 56
    product delivery, 56
    rework, 57
    seal the deal, 56
  keys, 54, 55
  top-notch, 54
  verbal, 58, 59
    body language, 59
    confidence, 59
    hard sell, 60
    language, 59
Confirmation bias, 117
Conflict management, 106
  BA, 107
    communication, 109, 110
    egocentrism, 109
    facilitators, 108
    nonnegotiable positions, 108
    similarities, 109
    underlying issues, 108

collaborators, 107
goals/objectives, project, 107
positions/opinions, 107
Creativity and problem-solving skills, 113
Credibility, 163
Cronyism/buddyism, 150

D

Data analysis, 32
Database knowledge, 31
Data mapping, 35, 36
Deception, 165
Decision-making, 91
   fear, 121
   information gap, 120
   long-term project, 120, 121
   maintains relationship, 120
   paralysis creation, 120
   project
      actors on same page, 119
      in motion, 119
   resolves problems, 119
   sunk costs, 121
   trust and credibility, 120
Documentation and writing skills, 60
   good grammar, 60
   language, 60

E

Egocentrism/self-centeredness, 109
Egoism, 93
   collaborative efforts, 98
   effects
      communication, 96
      conflicts, 96
      project progress, 95
   escalation, 98
   feedback, 97
   flawed logic/assumptions, 94
   hogging the limelight, 94
   personal issues, 95
   risk, 98
   role-play, 97, 98
   self-awareness, 94
   stakeholders, 95

tools, 98
   viewpoints, 94
Ego stroking, 76
Email management skills, 66
   attachments, 69
   content, 69
   effective, 67
   email chain, 68
   recipients, 69
   templates, 70
   visualization, 69
Emotional intelligence, 85
   challenges, 87
   confident and self-assured, 87
   empathy, 85
   importance
      build resilience, 88
      collaboration, 90
      cultivate relationships, 90
      decision-making, 91
      focus, 89
      learning opportunities, 89
      nuanced perspectives, 89
      open communications, 91
      persuasion, 91
      project actors, 92
      situations/actions, 89, 90
   lack of self-awareness, 88
   open minded, 86
   perspectives and insights, 86
   poor/inadequate, 87
   relationships, 88
   self-awareness, 85
   self-control, 85
   social skills, 86
Enterprise resource planning (ERP)
      systems, 41
Entity relationship diagrams (ERDs), 34, 35
Entrepreneurs, 124

F

Flattery, 76

G

Groupthink, 117
Guardrails, 160

H

Hack, BA
analytical abilities, 138
caveats, 141
fear, 143
humility and vulnerability, 142
impostor syndrome, 142
interfacing, team members, 139
leverage multiple information, 140
requirements scoping process, 140
review the documentation, 139
subject matter, 141
technology products, 142, 143
users and stakeholders, 139

I

Impostor syndrome, 142

International Institute of Business
Analysis (IIBA), 44

Interpersonal skills, 79–81

J

Joint application design (JAD), 70

K

Keep it simple, stupid (KISS), 102

L

Listening skills, 61
open mind, 62
paying attention, 62
practice, 63
presentation/ideas, 62, 63
staying engaged, 62

M

Management of meetings
action parties, 75
agenda, 71, 72
facilitator/presenter, 74
invitee, 72
need, 71
presentation, 72
purpose, 73
schedule, 73, 74

Managing meeting, 71

Mediation skills, 79

Meeting facilitation, 70

Microsoft Office Suite skills, 28

N, O

Negotiations and persuasive
abilities, 99
communication, 101
confidence, 101
expertise, 102
preparing battle plans, 101
trust and credibility, 100
user needs, 99, 100
users/stakeholders, 100

P

Problem-solving skills
active listening, 116
confirmation bias, 117
groupthink, 117
identifies the
problem, 116, 117
knowledge base, 116
open-minded, 117
openness/transparency, 116
project on track, 115

Process mapping, 135

Product testing, 36

Professionalism, 83

Programming languages, 43

Project Management Office
(PMO), 14, 38

Project management skills
list of tools, 39, 40
PMO, 38
project scope, 37
project timing, 38
status updates/reporting, 39
team management, 38

Prototyping, 37

Q

Quality assurance (QA), 36

R

Requirements Specification
  Document (RSD), 11
Resistance to change
  mind-sets/ways of working, 47, 48
  retraining/learning, 48
  transparency and visibility, 48
Root cause analysis (RCA), 114

S

Scripted Query Language (SQL), 28
Six sigma/lean management, 42
Sloppiness, 165, 166
Software Development Life Cycle
  (SDLC), 15, 25
  Agile/Scrum approach, 16, 17
  waterfall approach, 15, 16
Stakeholders
  accountability, 50
  documentation, 51
  pet project, 49
  wrecks, 50
Strategic thinking
  challenges, 123
  entrepreneurs, 124
  lifespan planning, 122
  mindset, 124
  organizational goals/objectives, 123
  requirements, 123, 124
  risk, mitigation, 122
Sunk costs, 121

T

Tact and diplomatic skills, 75
  importance, 76
  situations, 76
Technical certifications, 44
Technical writing, 29, 30
Tinkering waffler, 157

U

Use cases, 30, 31
User Acceptance Testing (UAT), 22

V

Visualization tools, 129, 135

W, X, Y

Waffling/indecision, 156, 161
Waffling, reasons
  buying time, 159
  changes, 159
  managerial incoherence, 158, 159
  managerial vacuums, 158
  minimal domain knowledge, 158
Waterfall approach, 15, 16
Waterfall *vs.* Agile Methodologies, 18
Web services/development, 42

Z

Zombie project, 150

CPSIA information can be obtained
at www.ICGtesting.com
Printed in the USA
BVHW040212301020
592204BV00017B/139